Mastering
Instruction

Mastering Instruction

Jack Martin

Simon Fraser University

ALLYN AND BACON, INC.

Boston London Sydney Toronto

Anonymous quotes throughout this text are taken from
written and oral statements given to the author by practicing or student teachers during the course of work at Simon
Fraser University.

Library of Congress Cataloging in Publication Data

Martin, Jack, 1950–
    Mastering instruction.
    Bibliography: p.
    Includes index.
    1. Teaching.   2. Teachers—Job stress.   I. Title.
LB1025.2.M364   1983   371.1'02   82–20778
ISBN 0-205-07879-6

Printed in the United States of America

10 9 8 7 6 5 4 3 2 1 88 87 86 85 84 83

Contents

Preface

The primary purpose of *Mastering Instruction* is to provide teachers and would-be teachers with information that will help them to cope effectively with the demands of an extremely difficult, yet ultimately important, profession. Modern society places a high premium on effective instruction, and teachers at all levels are finding themselves increasingly pressed by numerous and often conflicting demands for instructional excellence from a wide variety of societal groups and agencies. In such times, it is important that instructors understand the basic tools of effective instruction and how these tools can be implemented successfully in the delivery of sound instructional programs. With the ability to instruct effectively and to control personal reactions to professional stress, teaching is a richly rewarding vocation. *Mastering Instruction* considers both these abilities in detail.

This book describes a comprehensive model of teacher activity and counsels teachers in its practical utility through exploration of a wide range of instructional skills and strategies. Its approach to instruction is specific, practical, and implies a prudent deliberation of the entire process of instruction—what should occur before, during, and after a teacher's interaction with pupils, including what occurs inside the teacher's head when he or she contemplates the complex task of instruction. The process of instruction is depicted in a manner that emphasizes two crucial sets of actions: (1) teacher cognitions, and (2) teacher behaviors. *Teacher cognitions* include all the strategies that teachers employ in order to think about their instructional performances and to cope with the moment-to-moment, day-to-day pressures and exigencies of a difficult and excessively demanding profession. *Teacher behaviors* include all the skills, strategies, and styles that instructors employ in order to assist pupils in the vitally important process of learning. By looking at these two actions, *Mastering Instruction* places joint emphasis on what teachers do and what teachers think about what they do. Both are seen as active processes through which teachers encourage and foster student learning in the classroom. In this sense, *Mastering Instruction* takes a cognitive-behavioral approach.

This book attempts to specify as clearly and precisely as possible the exact skills required for successful execution of each phase of the instructional process. With the exception of Chapter 1, each chapter contains subsections relevant to the particular topics discussed and concludes with *Questions and Responses* and *Suggested Activities* sections, which engage the reader in active, ongoing dialogue and practice activities aimed at increasing the meaningfulness of the subject matter.

Before turning to Chapter 1, two related disclaimers are in order. The first disclaimer is that, while this book specifies and describes the essential ingredients of instructional activity, it does not ensure the acquisition of these skills. This is so because the successful acquisition of any skill requires specification of the skill, appropriate practice of the skill under realistic conditions, and precise feedback concerning such practice. Although this book recommends and describes skills, it leaves to the reader the job of practicing these skills in real classroom contexts and of arranging for (and welcoming) constructive feedback aimed at improving performance of the skills.

The second disclaimer is that there is no "magic" in the instructional model presented. Learning to instruct is a difficult undertaking that requires a high level of commitment to hard work. There is no substitute for well-organized, efficient practice. Excellence in instruction results more from ongoing, active effort to improve than from any secret formula that may be imbibed passively to produce miraculous results. The potential effectiveness of any instructional philosophy, method, or approach can never be realized without active, dedicated effort.

Finally, a quick word about how to use this book. While it describes instructional skills, readers are free to pick and choose the ones they will incorporate into their own teaching repertoires and the ones they will reject. This is the way it should be, since each of us has slightly different instructional strengths and weaknesses. Nonetheless, the timing of such decisions is extremely important. In most cases, a decision to discard a particular skill should be made only after it has been studied, practiced conscientiously, and found to be incompatible with a particular teacher or instructional context. In this way, the teacher can ensure that decisions to accept or reject specific skills are true decisions based on accurate information and the knowledge of personal experience. To this end, the reader is entreated to keep an open mind initially and to exercise an informed decision-making faculty.

The work of producing a book like this requires the efforts of many people in addition to the author. At Simon Fraser University, I have been aided by the ideas and comments of Peter Coleman, John F. Ellis, Bryan A. Hiebert, Ronald W. Marx, and Philip H. Winne. The production of initial and final manuscripts could not have been accomplished without the assistance of Pat MacDonald and Wyn Martin. Finally, I am deeply indebted to the instruction I received from John McLeish.

J.M.

1

Mastering Instruction

"I often think how fortunate I've been in choosing to spend my working life as a teacher. I suppose everyone derives satisfaction and pleasure from doing a job well. However, I doubt very much that many other jobs afford the sense of accomplishment that comes from having a direct hand in the learning and development of so many young people. Just knowing that I have knowledge and skills that permit me to assist my students in learning new things and discovering new abilities gives me tremendous satisfaction.

"Oh sure, there are always days when things are a bit hectic for one reason or another. But generally I feel that I can handle anything that occurs if I simply stay calm and use the skills that I possess. Yes, teaching has been very good to me. My experiences as a teacher have taught me so many things."

"When I first started teaching, seven years ago, I was excited and enthusiastic about the career I had chosen. I recognized how important it was, and while I was anxious about how I would do, I looked forward to the challenge of helping youngsters in the primary grades learn to read, write, think, and enjoy these new abilities and the increased personal esteem and power that go with them. Each day at work was thrilling, and each night I was filled with new ideas I wanted to employ in planning the next day's action.

"Now, seven years later, I don't have that enthusiasm any more. In fact, it's all I can do to drag myself into the classroom. My grand visions are just memories that seem far away and rather silly. Who did I think I was that I could do all those things? I can't really put my finger on what has changed. I guess maybe a lot of things. At any rate, I don't enjoy what I'm doing, and I can't see what I can do about it, or what alternatives I have open to me at this stage. I feel trapped and, worst of all, I feel dishonest—like an imposter—every time I look at one of those young, eager faces. It really is frustrating, the way I now behave. But I can't do anything about it, and I really don't think there is much that anyone can do in my situation. This is the way it is for me."

"There was a time when I never thought I'd feel really comfortable in a classroom. When I first started teaching, I got pretty anxious before each class. I don't know why, but I suppose, in retrospect, that I wasn't sure of what to expect from the students or from myself. Thinking of those times now, it's hard for me to believe that I actually used to react that way. At this moment, I can't think of anything at which I'm happier and more relaxed than teaching.

"My experiences really prove that a person can learn to teach well, even if you're not an instant success. I've learned so many things and acquired so many skills during the three years that I've taught junior high school. I guess that learning all of these things has made me less anxious when I walk into a classroom of learners. At any rate, I look forward to each class and to the challenges it will bring."

"I don't mind admitting that I'm getting so anxious about my job that I can hardly stand it. It really bothers me that I feel so incompetent. I've been teaching grade 10 students for two years now, and even though I really want to teach well and try to improve, I still seem to be a failure. Half the time I just don't know what to say or do. I know the curriculum backwards and forwards, but I can't seem to get it across to the kids so that they enjoy it like I do.

"You know, it really makes me mad that I haven't learned how to teach despite all my hard work and effort. I feel really cheated by the teacher training program I took. Almost none of that stuff is useful to me now. And as far as learning anything from the rest of the teachers here, forget it. Most of them teach as badly as I do or worse and seem not to recognize it; or if they do, they pretend that the system just won't let them do any better."

The foregoing statements are very different in the kinds of attitudes, feelings, and thoughts they convey. The apathy, blaming, and insecurity evident in two of the statements are in direct contrast to the enjoyment, optimism, and enthusiasm evident in the other two statements. Recent examinations of teachers' job satisfaction and professional stress have revealed large differences in the reactions of individual teachers to the demands and circumstances of their work (e.g., Kyriacou and Sutcliffe, 1978; Youngs, 1978). For most contemporary teachers, teaching is a fulfilling, exciting profession. Unfortunately for a growing minority of teachers, anxiety and frustration are constant vocational companions.

The term *teacher burnout* (e.g., Youngs, 1978) has been coined to describe the negative emotional and attitudinal exhaustion felt by teachers who are unable to cope effectively with the demands of their professional roles. These demands are often exacerbated by factors such as increasing workloads, larger class sizes, criticism from parents and others, rapid curriculum changes, and a gradual shift of instructional control from teachers to trustees and government bureaucrats. While most observers see these factors as general causes of teacher burnout, such causal emphasis on broad social and political factors does little to improve the ability of individual teachers to prepare for, fulfill, and cope with the demands of a difficult, stressful, and vital profession (Coates and Thoresen, 1976; Kyriacou and Sutcliffe, 1978). Such explanations for teacher burnout also fail to explain why most teachers continue to have a positive attitude toward their work. Clearly, some teachers are able to master the numerous demands of instruction better than other teachers. The things that teachers do in classrooms and the ways in which they think about these actions are major determinants of instructional success and professional satisfaction. It is not difficult to imagine that the different thoughts and actions reported by teachers who offered the earlier statements are likely to have very different effects on the instructional experiences of the teachers reporting them.

INSTRUCTIONAL COGNITIONS, BEHAVIORS, AND STRESS

The eminent psychologist Albert Bandura (1977a, 1977b, 1978, 1980) provides a theoretical framework for the interactions among *situations, behaviors,* and *cognitions.* This framework helps us to understand the experiences of contemporary teachers. Bandura's model implies that what we do, what we think about what we do, and the situations in which we perform can influence each other in a reciprocal manner. Thus, a teacher who has just met with an angry and unfair parent (situation) may think that teaching is unrewarding (cognition) and may fail to put sufficient effort into the next classroom lesson (behavior). Conversely, a teacher who lacks instructional skills (behavior) may find that his or her students learn slowly and react negatively (situation); thus, the teacher may come to think that the students are not motivated and that nothing can be done about this (cognition). The same teacher, experiencing negative feedback from students, may read an article about the ingratitude of modern children (situation), which reinforces the belief that students are incorrigible brats (cognition), and leads the teacher to adopt an angry classroom demeanor in addition to the basic lack of instructional skills (behavior). Each factor (situation, cognition, behavior) has the ability to influence and be influenced by the other factors. It is possible to see the vast potential for the development of vicious downward spirals in which teacher attitudes (cognitions), teacher classroom actions (behaviors), and feedback from students, parents, administrators, and others (situations) all hit record lows. The natural result of such a downward spiral is stress and a weakening of personal abilities to cope with stress in positive, rational ways.

Fortunately, Bandura's model is informative also with respect to the amelioration of such spirals and the accompanying experiences of stress and disaffection. It is clear from Bandura's theory that, if an unproductive cycle of situations, cognitions, and behaviors develops, the only way to stop or reverse the degenerative direction of this cycle is to alter one or more of the factors contributing to it. Situational factors typically are less directly controlled by an individual than are personal cognitions and behaviors. Therefore, any change usually must "begin at home" with the purposeful and systematic alteration of the ways in which the teacher performs (instructional behaviors) and thinks about his or her performance (instructional cognitions). While this idea seems to imply that teachers are their own worst enemies, great care must be exercised in drawing such an inference. If the intention of such a statement is to say that teachers who are experiencing job-related stress are totally responsible for their own problems, such an implication is clearly in error. External situational factors are always associated with stress of this kind. Varied and conflicting demands on the classroom teacher from pupils, parents, school administrators, social groups, government agencies, and public media are major contributors to teacher stress. Indeed, it may be the case that such demands, while usually well intentioned, do much more to intensify existing educational difficulties than to reduce them. Nonetheless, although Bandura's model fully recognizes the tremendous effects of external situational factors, it also tells us that such factors are mediated by other, more personally controlled factors of individual thought and action.

Teachers who possess strong instructional skills and who judge themselves to be effective in their instructional roles are much less affected by adverse situational factors than are teachers who possess weaker instructional skills or who are uncertain about their effectiveness in the classroom. For example, a teacher of the former kind may react to the criticism of a parent by inviting the parent into the classroom to observe instruction firsthand so as to comprehend the teacher's position better and to gain a greater appreciation of the teacher's skills and abilities. This might lead to increased support from the parent and from the segments of the immediate community in which the parent is influential. On the other hand, a teacher who lacks instructional skill or the conviction that he or she is effective may engage the same parent in a vitriolic dispute and reap a return of increased parental and community disapproval. A consideration of the relative potential for teacher stress that resides in each of these two scenarios illustrates the substantial contributions of individual teacher behaviors and cognitions to instructional stress and the ability to cope with it.

The advantage of realizing that individual thoughts and actions have a direct role in determining job satisfaction, effectiveness, and stress reactions lies in two facts. First, personal behaviors and thoughts are more directly controllable by the individual teacher than are external, situational factors. Second, when individual thoughts and behaviors are controlled in a positive manner, they can influence situational factors in equally positive ways. Therefore, teachers who wish to master their instructional roles should place joint emphasis on what and how they think about what they do (instructional cognitions) and on what they actually do (instructional behaviors).

A MODEL OF INSTRUCTION

The universe of instructional cognitions and behaviors is enormous. Productive examination of this universe requires a conceptual lens through which meaningful observations can be made. The model of instructional cognitions and behaviors depicted in Figure 1.1 provides such a lens. Instructional cognitions and instructional behaviors are associated directly with the determination of instructional effectiveness and stress. Fortunately, both cognitions and behaviors may be subjected to relatively direct control by individual teachers. This is not to deny the powerful effects that external situational (e.g., social, cultural, political) factors exert upon instructional stress and effectiveness; rather, my intention is to emphasize the factors that individual teachers can control and master directly.

Mastering instruction requires accurate cognitive comprehension and efficient performance of a wide variety of instructional behaviors throughout the entire process of instruction. Some of these behaviors (*preactive*) are employed before actual interactions between teacher and students take place, while others (*interactive*) are associated directly with what a teacher does in direct interactions with students. Still another set of instructional behaviors (*evaluation*) accompanies and often follows the interactive phase of instruction. The purposeful orchestration and execution of all these instructional behaviors in ways

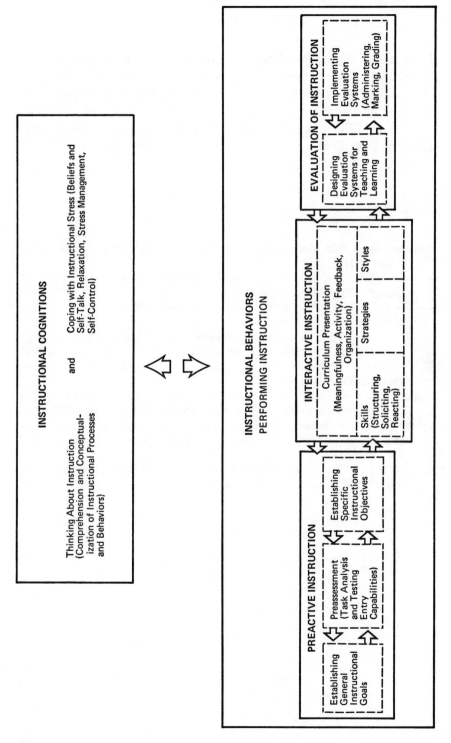

FIGURE 1.1

that promote the intended student learning is what instruction is all about. This book is meant to help teachers seize control of their instructional efforts (literally, to master the variables that contribute to effective, unstressful instruction) by clearly depicting all types of instructional behaviors and by counseling instructors about the ways in which they might think most profitably about these behaviors.

REFERENCES

Bandura, A. 1977a. *Social Learning Theory.* Englewood Cliffs, N.J.: Prentice-Hall.

——. 1977b. Self-efficacy: Toward a unifying theory of behavioral change. *Psychological Review* 84: 191–215.

——. 1978. The self system in reciprocal determinism. *American Psychologist* 33: 344–358.

——. Self-referent thought: the development of self-efficacy. In *Cognitive Social Development: Frontiers and Possible Futures,* edited by J.H. Flavell and L.D. Ross. New York: Cambridge University Press, 1980.

Coates, T.J., and Thoresen, C.E. 1976. Teacher anxiety: a review with recommendations. *Review of Educational Research* 46: 159–184.

Kyriacou, C., and Sutcliffe, J. 1978. Teacher stress: prevalence, sources and symptoms. *British Journal of Educational Psychology* 48: 159–167.

Youngs, B.B. 1978. Anxiety and stress—how they affect teachers, teaching. *NASSP Bulletin* 62: 78–83.

2

Coping with Instructional Stress

Teacher burnout, teacher stress, and *teaching anxiety* are all terms that are used to depict difficulties experienced by teachers in coping with the heavy and often conflicting demands of their profession. *Mastering Instruction* presents a cognitive-behavioral approach to instruction that is based on the central notion that instructional stress and instructional effectiveness are determined largely by the instructional cognitions and behaviors of the individual teacher. Although situational factors and pressures obviously affect these phenomena, the best way to overcome instructional stress is to master the sets of cognitions and behaviors that define effective instruction.

Instructional cognitions can be divided into two categories: (1) thoughts relating to the comprehension and conceptualization of specific instructional processes and behaviors, and (2) personal thoughts and judgments about oneself and one's capabilities in the overall task of instruction. The first set of cognitions is associated closely with the specific instructional behaviors executed at each phase of the instructional process. These cognitions cannot be considered profitably apart from related instructional behaviors; I will examine these cognitions in the chapters that follow. It is the second category of cognitions—the general, personal beliefs about one's instructional effectiveness and capabilities—that I will examine in this chapter. In relation to Bandura's model of behavioral, cognitive, and situational factors (see Chapter 1), we can see these general cognitions as factors that pervasively influence instructional performances and situations.

BELIEFS AND SELF-TALK

Learning to cope with the stress factors associated with contemporary teaching is not simply a matter of skillful instructional behavior; rather, it is related directly to how teachers *think about, perceive,* and *cognitively label* the pressures and stress factors they encounter. These cognitions are associated directly with basic *beliefs* held by individual teachers. These beliefs may center on the nature of instruction, may include assessments of individual instructional abilities, or may relate to the nature and meaning of the experience of anxiety or stress.

The ways in which we think about situations and our performance in these situations can have a direct effect on the stress we experience. More specifically, stress/anxiety reactions are determined largely by private thoughts in the form of *internal self-statements*— i.e., the things we say to ourselves about situations we encounter and about our performance in these situations (Ellis, 1962; Meichenbaum, 1977). Some internal self-statements are so pervasive and frequent that they become basic beliefs that guide our conduct. When these beliefs are illogical, misleading, or inaccurate, the constant repetition of them in the form of *self-talk* can be responsible for maintaining stress/ anxiety reactions. For example, a teacher who thinks that he or she is being treated unfairly by the principal of the school may or may not experience stress as a result of this thought. However, if the teacher insists on this perceived injustice by repeating it internally over and over again, or if he or she combines this thought with a more basic belief (e.g., "People should always be fair to me, and it is absolutely intolerable when they are not"), the likelihood that stress/anxiety will occur on a continuing basis is greatly increased. External situations or circumstances tend not to maintain anxiety and stress. Although such situations may initiate a stress response, it is irrational, defeatist self-talk that often gives rise to disruptive, extended stress reactions.

The general cognitions or beliefs that are associated with defeatist self-talk (and, therefore, stress) have been studied extensively in recent years (Beck, 1976; Ellis, 1975; Meichenbaum, 1977). When these beliefs are transposed into the instructional arena, a number of commonly held, disruptive beliefs about instruction, teachers, and stress emerge.

1. *"If you're the anxious type, teaching isn't your game."* This belief occurs in a variety of forms. It is concerned essentially with the notion that anxiety and disposition to stress are personality traits that are fixed and cannot be altered. It is hard to imagine a more defeatist belief than this one. Imagine the plight of a teacher who wants to make teaching a career, is experiencing a bit of anxiety about a new course, and who holds this basic belief. For this individual, every anxious moment becomes a traumatic vocational dilemma. The belief that anxiety is a personality characteristic can result in long periods of redundant soul-searching, self-doubt, and tension.

Fortunately, the consensus among stress and behavior experts (Bandura, 1977; Meichenbaum, 1977; Kanfer and Goldstein, 1980) is that we all experience stress or anxiety from time to time and in certain situations; stress is a natural part of living. All teachers experience stress. The ability to live successfully with professional stress must be *learned.* It is not a natural ability that is given to some and denied others. Some teachers have learned active methods of handling stress; others have not. One of the most effective ways to avoid or cope with professional stress is to discard beliefs such as "If you're the anxious type, there is nothing you can do about it except get out of the teaching profession."

2. *"If you experience any stress at all, this is a bad thing that you should be very concerned about."* This belief is replete with defeatist notions. It views stress and anxiety as unnatural and indicates that something is wrong with the person who experiences them. It also implies that one must master any experience of stress so completely that it never occurs again.

Once more, the evidence is against this belief (Barrios and Shigetomi, 1979; Meichenbaum, 1977). The assumption generally supported in the professional literature on stress and anxiety is that *active coping* is a more effective approach to successful stress/anxiety management than is complete mastery. It would be nice if stress/anxiety reactions never occurred. However, attempts to eradicate them completely have been less effective than attempts to live with stress/anxiety factors so that their debilitating effects are minimized. Coping with stress does not remove stress factors, nor does it totally remove an individual's immediate reaction to them. Good "copers" use initial stress reactions as cues to engage in active coping strategies that can successfully counteract the primary debilitating, negative personal consequences of stress. Learning to cope with stress makes much more sense than trying to master stress completely. Attempts at mastery are likely to fail, since any evidence of even minimal anxiety or stress indicates failure to master. Conversely, for individuals equipped with effective coping strategies, any sign of a minimal stress/anxiety response simply cues the use of these strategies to avoid further upset.

Because active coping with stress is a learned ability, it demands hard work. Solving the personal and professional problems associated with stress/anxiety demands considerable individual effort and commitment. This is another major reason for the inappropriateness of the mastery model for reducing stress/anxiety. This model assumes that stress can be dealt with passively, through some kind of externalized cure or magic solution. It is doubtful, however, that stress/anxiety reactions are ever managed successfully without direct, active effort by the individual. In short, there is no easy way around professional stress, but there are effective means of actively managing and coping with it.

3. *"Every student, colleague, and parent I come in contact with must like me and approve of everything I am doing; otherwise, I am failing as a teacher."* This belief is so blatantly irrational that most teachers would deny it out of hand. Unfortunately, such a quick dismissal is often inconsistent with the degree of upset experienced whenever anyone does disapprove of one's instructional efforts or viewpoints. Whether or not we like it, most of us accept at least some of the logic contained in this belief. This acceptance often places us in a no-win position, since complete approval from all students, colleagues, or parents is never possible. There are just too many equally plausible but different opinions about instructional matters ever to expect such total support. Probably the best that we can do in this regard is to learn to be articulate in explaining our own position and

methods. It is possible for people to disagree in a rational manner and to continue to work together.

The fact that some individuals disapprove of some things you do does not necessarily imply that they are unable to like other things about you or your methods. On the other hand, the fact that an occasional student or colleague simply does not like you (which happens to everyone from time to time) is not a major catastrophe in and of itself. Effective instruction and learning are not totally precluded by the absence of a friendly relationship between a teacher and all his or her students and colleagues.

4. *"It's a terrible shame that I can't teach in the ideal situation."* This belief can be defeatist both because of its extreme view and because of its potential for precluding constructive actions. It is entirely reasonable for a teacher to wish to teach in as supportive a situation as possible. However, the absence of a highly supportive situation is not necessarily a terrible shame. It may be inconvenient in any number of ways and may prevent teaching from being a totally pleasant experience, but it is seldom terrible.

The real problem with this belief, however, is that it may be accepted and reinforced with frequent self-talk that expresses it in various ways. The teacher may spend so much time dwelling on the inadequacies of a situation that he or she will totally ignore its positive aspects and the possible avenues for improvement. Once again, most instructional situations are affected by the teacher's instructional behaviors and cognitions. When these behaviors and cognitions are allowed to become negative and defeatist, the potential for altering situations in positive directions is severely limited.

5. *"The whole teaching system needs to be changed, and until it is there is little I can do."* This belief is associated closely with the preceding one, but it goes one step further in limiting constructive instructional cognitions and actions. Not only can it lead the teacher to negative inactivity, but it also appears to justify such inactivity by implying that the causes of apathy lie in external factors completely outside the teacher's control. Blaming all of one's problems on "the system" may be reassuring in the short term; however, in the long run this approach fails to recognize that, as part of the educational system, each teacher is responsible for fulfilling the functions associated with his or her position.

It simply is not true that individual teachers are powerless in the face of the system. By acquiring a broad range of effective instructional skills and the ability to justify the use of such skills, teachers can accomplish a great deal. There usually are ways to do a job effectively, regardless of a few external constraints.

6. *"I must be the perfect teacher and never make a mistake."* This belief also is blantantly irrational and unrealistic but surprisingly common among teachers (although it is seldom expressed quite so candidly). The real danger that emanates from this belief is that it precludes experimentation with a variety of instructional skills and methods. Such experimentation plays a crucial role in learning to teach. Without it, teachers may fall into stereotypic, inflexible instructional strategies from which they are afraid to deviate for fear of committing some terrible instructional error. Consequently, many teachers who hold this belief grasp tightly to the first one or two instructional methods with which they achieve any degree of success. Many teachers do not alter their limited approaches no matter how long they stay in the profession. This is not to say that limited instructional strategies are necessarily ineffective. However, they can become extremely boring to the teacher; this in turn can become a major contributor to job dissatisfaction and professional stress.

Every teacher inevitably makes mistakes. No single error in interacting with a student or group of students is capable by itself of resulting in continuing instructional failure. If we learn from our mistakes and do not delight in deprecating ourselves for our natural imperfections, we can discover new insights about the process of instruction. Such insights may well enhance future instructional efforts.

7. *"I'm not a natural teacher and will never do very well in this profession."* This belief assumes that some of us are naturally endowed with the ingredients necessary for successful instruction and others are not. Such a belief may be harmless if a teacher sees himself or herself as one of the chosen few. However, even in this case the belief may create problems by implying that successful instruction cannot be learned. While it may be true that some people, as a result of the kind and quality of their experiences, are better prepared to teach than others, instructional skills can be acquired with the right mix of information, practice, and feedback. Spending time wondering whether

or not you are a "natural" teacher is likely to prove unproductive and may induce needless stress.

The general cognitions described in the preceding paragraphs illustrate the types of beliefs that can give rise to defeatist, stress-inducing self-talk. Not only can such beliefs result in stress, but they also can reduce the stressed individual's capacity to cope with the stress/anxiety they experience. While the external, situational factors that initiate professional stress among educators are numerous, these factors alone do not maintain high levels of debilitating stress. Rather, it is the way in which each teacher perceives, thinks about, labels, and interprets these factors that can create true stress problems (cf. Ellis, 1962; Meichenbaum, 1977).

As an illustration of how beliefs and self-talk can contribute to professional stress, consider the relative potential for stress reactions inherent in the following two sets of self-statements.

> "I don't want to go to the school today. I can't stand the thought of it. I just can't cope with the kids anymore. What am I going to do? I'm going nuts over this."
>
> versus
>
> "The school and kids aren't going to make me go crazy. What's really bothering me is all this nonsense I'm telling myself. If I stop this silliness, I'll be okay. It's my stupid, irrational ideas that are bothering me, not the kids or the school. If I stop hurting myself, the school situation can't hurt me. I'm a good teacher, and all I need to do is to relax and enjoy myself."

RELAXATION

Coping with stress is an active process that requires effort and some basic tools and skills. One of the most important skills for coping with stress is the ability to relax deeply and at will. Skill at relaxing can have the dual effect of reducing existing stress/anxiety and preparing the way for positive actions that are antithetical to a continuation of debilitating stress. There are numerous relaxation programs and systems that are readily available to teachers and others (e.g., Jacobson,

1938; Wolpe and Lazarus, 1966; Hiebert, 1980). Whether or not you currently are experiencing anxiety or stress, the basic skill of relaxation is a useful one.

Most relaxation training programs consist of a series of scripted instructions that ask the participant alternately to tense and relax a wide range of specific muscle groups located throughout the body. *Relaxation is clearly recognized as the opposite sensation of tension.* Instructions typically begin by asking participants to follow directions promptly and accurately and by suggesting that participants make themselves as comfortable as possible (e.g., lying on a carpeted floor, sitting in a comfortable chair with adequate head support). The training continues with instructions to clench or tense a particular area of the body (e.g., the right hand) for a short time (five seconds or so). Instructions are then given to relax this part of the body for the same length of time and to study carefully the disappearance of tension and the physical sensation of deep muscle relaxation, which now is apparent in the previously tensed area. The participant usually tenses and relaxes each muscle group two or three times in succession before applying the technique to another body area. In a half-hour to an hour training period, the muscle groups associated with the following body parts are tensed and relaxed in a sequence similar to that described here: right hand (tense by clenching the fist); left hand; right wrist (tense by bending backward and pointing fingers upward); left wrist; both arms (tense biceps by bringing hands to shoulders); both shoulders (tense by shrugging upward towards ears); forehead (tense by wrinkling); eyes (tense by shutting tightly); tongue (tense by pressing against roof of mouth); lips (tense by pushing together); head (tense by pushing back against floor or chair); neck (tense by burying chin in chest); chest (tense by taking a deep breath and holding it); stomach (tense by "sucking in"), buttocks (tense by pushing seat down hard); thighs (tense by stretching legs out straight and lifting both feet off the ground); toes and feet (tense by pointing toes upward toward face and then curling them downward). Once each muscle group has been alternately tensed and relaxed, participants are asked to scan their bodies for any sensation of tension and to eliminate any remaining tensions immediately by relaxing the affected muscle group more deeply.

After several repetitions of this or a similar training sequence over a period of several days, it is possible to learn to relax more and more easily. Gradually, by going through the relaxation training sequence more and more briefly, you should be able to obtain a good relaxation response simply by telling yourself to relax.

There is nothing mysterious about relaxation training, and most people, particularly those engaged in extremely demanding professions, should develop some means of relaxing at will. Solitary walks, brief isolation in a quiet area, or quick catnaps are common ways of relaxing; however, these techniques are usually more difficult to access in the middle of professional undertakings than is a well-conditioned, self-controlled relaxation response. Once again, many excellent relaxation programs and scripts are available. There also is nothing wrong with constructing an individual relaxation training system on the basis of the tensing-relaxing principles described here. Regardless of how you acquire relaxation skills, the important consideration is to practice the relaxation response sufficiently to permit its immediate and effective use in stressful situations.

STRESS MANAGEMENT

Recently, a number of cognitive-behavioral psychologists and educators (see Barrios and Shigetomi, 1979) have combined the use of relaxation for reducing stress with insights gained from studies of the ways in which personal belief systems and self-talk influence stress reactions. The result of this synthesis has been a variety of strategies for stress management that emphasize three basic processes: (1) recognizing defeatist self-talk and beliefs; (2) using relaxation to interrupt such self-talk, together with the stress/anxiety it produces; and (3) promoting constructive action through the use of positive, enhancing self-talk. These steps can be employed to create a useful, practical, and relatively simple approach that can be used to manage instructional stress.

Recognizing Defeatist Self-Talk

The first phase in a cognitive-behavioral strategy for coping with instructional stress involves *recognition* of defeatist self-talk and beliefs.

Many examples of general self-defeating cognitions were discussed earlier in this chapter. The recognition phase of stress management is concerned with techniques that teachers can employ to "catch" specific defeatist self-statements associated with their own personal stress reactions.

Recognition of defeatist self-statements is best accomplished by examining the situations in which we experience stress or anxiety (usually beginning with relatively mild stress-inducing situations). What do we say to ourselves before, during, and after such experiences? (Note that the things we tell ourselves on such occasions may not be delivered in easily recognized sentences or phrases. Vague feelings and experiences of "simply going blank" may obscure any discernable self-talk. However, with some probing and increased attention to our internal dialogue, it usually is possible to get at some of the basic messages we are sending to ourselves.) Once self-talk in stressful situations has been examined in this fashion, it is important to search for typical categories of statements that seem to be particularly debilitating—that is, statements that often lead to ineffective actions, frustration, depression, panic, withdrawal, avoidance/escape, or loss of temper. Once you have identified such examples of debilitating self-talk, it is useful to try to monitor their use in similar situations.

What happens when these thoughts occur? The kind of introspective probing described in the preceding paragraph can help teachers to become thoroughly familiar with the ways in which their patterns of defeatist self-talk are related to stress/anxiety reactions. Examination of some of the more common forms of defeatist instructional beliefs described earlier can help orient teachers to the kinds of cognitive themes associated with stress reactions. However, although some defeatist beliefs are widely held, the exact form of the self-talk is likely to be quite idiosyncratic. The task during this initial phase of stress management is for instructors to probe their own self-thoughts during stress/anxiety experiences to determine the precise self-talk patterns associated with their personal stress responses.

Once the teacher has probed and recognized what appear to be significant stress-related self-talk patterns, he or she can double-check the validity of the causal connection between these patterns and their stress reactions. This can be done by checking self-talk patterns before, during, and after relaxing, comfortable, or enjoyable situations.

The patterns of self-talk discovered during these nonstressful times should differ in recognizable ways from those recorded during times of stress. This checking exercise is useful for ensuring the discovery of truly debilitating self-talk themes. It also is useful for providing an understanding of alternative self-statements that are associated with relaxation and calm. Such knowledge is particularly useful in the final phases of the stress management strategy.

At the end of the first phase of stress management, the teacher should understand clearly and be able to recognize key defeatist self-statements associated with situations that produce instructional stress. This recognition should be tuned so finely that the individual is able to predict incipient stress/anxiety by recognizing the first signs of defeatist self-talk.

Stopping Defeatist Self-Talk

The second phase of instructional stress management is concerned with the *removal* of defeatist self-talk. Since such cognitive talk is a primary factor that contributes to professional stress, it follows that its removal or cessation should be associated with a partial reduction in the feeling of stress (see Meichenbaum, 1977; Wolpe, 1958). Once a teacher recognizes the first signs of debilitating self-talk associated with stress, he or she should apply active coping responses that will effectively terminate such talk and the resulting stress.

There are essentially two processes involved in effectively stopping defeatist self-talk. The first is the establishment of a powerful internal cue that can be self-delivered at the first sign of debilitating self-talk. This cue is intended to interrupt the defeatist thought pattern momentarily. A good method of establishing such an internal cue is to use the word STOP in the following manner (Wolpe, 1958): Whenever you are alone and find yourself engaging in self-defeating thoughts, scream "STOP!" as loudly as you can. Reduce the volume of this interruptive technique gradually over successive uses until the STOP command becomes a subvocal, internal interrupter. The effect of the STOP command, if properly delivered, should be to disrupt the flow of defeatist self-talk momentarily.

The brief interruption in negative cognitions brought about by the STOP technique provides the opportunity for the stressed individual to engage in a strong relaxation response. (This response should have been acquired previously using techniques and training procedures similar to those described earlier in this chapter.) Relaxation is then maintained for a brief period, during which all physical tensions are removed from the body and cognitive activity is similarly calm and pleasant.

Promoting Positive Self-Talk and Action

In phase one of the instructional stress management strategy, the teacher recognizes defeatist self-talk. In phase two, he or she uses the initial signs of such talk as a cue for engaging in thought-stopping and relaxation responses that terminate negative thought patterns associated with stress. The third phase in the strategy is based on the idea that, if derogatory, debilitating forms of self-talk lead to stress/anxiety reactions, then positive, enhancing forms of self-talk should lead to a reduction in stress/anxiety reactions (Meichenbaum, 1977).

By carefully probing internal cognitive talk patterns that occur during periods of enjoyment, relaxation, or contentment, it is possible for an individual to get some idea of the kinds of positive self-talk he or she can use to reduce further or remove stress reactions. Such positive self-statements may be used after the temporary cessation of defeatist self-talk brought about by thought stopping and relaxation. This series of *coping self-statements* can be used (1) to prepare for major stress situations, (2) confront and handle these situations, (3) cope with the feeling of being overwhelmed, or (4) reinforce oneself for effective coping.

The following selection of positive coping statements illustrates the general kinds of self-statements that the teacher can employ during phase three.

1. *Preparing for stress situations*
   - "Now that I'm relaxed, let me think about what I have to do tomorrow."
   - "I know I can do all right if I just remain calm and develop a good, solid plan of action."

- "There's no sense getting upset now, since that will just prevent me from doing good instructional planning."
- "If my plan is strong, the chances for a positive evaluation from my principal will be very good."

2. *Confronting stress situations*
    - "O.K., here we go. I'm well prepared and I can do the job."
    - "Relax, I'm in control. I'll just take a deep, slow breath."
    - "Just take it one step at a time. I've introduced the lesson and stated some clear objectives. So far, so good."
    - "If Johnny doesn't answer, I'll ask Sally whether she can help him out. Yes, that's what I can do. No need to panic when I know what to do."

3. *Coping with feeling overwhelmed*
    - "O.K., I'm getting a bit anxious here. No big deal, I can manage it. It's only natural to feel a bit anxious."
    - "This is a bit difficult right now. Just hang in there, stay calm, and give the students time to answer."
    - "Just stop all this silliness. Don't beat yourself."
    - "Keep the focus on the present; what is it that I want to do now?"
    - "To heck with Mr. Phelps. My job is to teach these kids, and that's what I'm going to do."

4. *Reinforcing effective coping*
    - "Hey, it worked. I did a great job."
    - "I didn't get so anxious that I couldn't prepare myself, and even when I got a bit uptight during the lesson I really hung in there."
    - "My strategy of just stopping the nonsense, doing a quick relax, and talking positively to myself really worked."
    - "I'm really on top of it now."

Once you have developed a set of positive self-statements, you should practice them (i.e., recite them internally in a variety of forms) until they become virtually automatic. You can practice them initially while you are relaxing at home. You can then move on to recite them as you imagine the stress situations for which they have been designed. Finally, practice should involve covert repetition of the statements during real-life stress situations (e.g., classrooms, staff meetings, parent interviews). To ensure every possible chance for success, it is a good idea to graduate practice from mildly stressful to severely stressful situations, and from brief intervals of stress contact to more extended ones.

Summary

The instructional stress management strategy described here is a cognitive-behavioral approach that teachers can use to cope actively with instructional stress. It assumes that teachers who use the strategy already have skills in understanding the stress-inducing effects of defeatist self-talk and beliefs, and that they have skills in relaxation. The three steps in the strategy are (1) prompt recognition of defeatist self-talk, (2) use of such recognition as a cue to apply thought-stopping and relaxation responses to interrupt defeatist talk and the accompanying stress, and (3) substitution of positive, enhancing self-talk patterns for defeatist cognitions. While the acquisition of these skills can take a good deal of time and effort, once they are acquired they can be employed in a very brief time span (five to thirty seconds) and can be used covertly in almost any stressful situation. Eventually, they can become so automatic that the teacher can use them as readily as he or she would scan a lesson plan during a lesson or scan a classroom to locate the source of a minor disturbance.

SELF-CONTROL AND PROFESSIONAL GROWTH

This chapter has been concerned predominantly with general instructional cognitions (i.e., personal thoughts and judgments about oneself and one's capabilities in relation to instruction) regarding the creation and management of instructional stress. The remainder of the book will outline a variety of instructional behaviors and cognitions that relate specifically to the execution of various phases of the instructional process. In a very real sense, the entire book is intended as a blueprint for professional growth. By acquiring and constantly working to improve the skills and strategies described here, both preservice and in-service teachers can grow and develop in ways that continuously enhance their personal and instructional effectiveness and self-image.

Acquisition of the numerous behaviors and cognitions that lead to effective instruction demands hard work and constant, dedicated effort. There are no magic ways to grow as a teacher. Professional events, special conferences, workshops, and professional reading are all useless unless teachers make the ultimate decision to work hard to improve basic instructional skills and strategies. The following quotation, taken from the personal log of a practicing teacher, sums it up this way:

> If you truly want to improve and grow, you must accept the responsibility for engendering such changes yourself. Blaming others for preventing your own growth and development is nonsense. You control your own growth. In recognizing this truth, you must also recognize that your attempts will never be perfect, and that part of growing effectively is learning to live with your own human limitations within a world in which no solutions are ever complete or permanent. Nonetheless, it is always possible to gain contentment by working consistently to improve your own teaching skills and strategies within these limits.

While it may sound trite, it is always the case that the credit for any improvement in individual instructional skills and effectiveness ultimately must go to the teacher. It is important not to overlook this fact, since an important part of reducing professional stress and increasing instructional effectiveness lies in the ability of each teacher to *self-reward*. That is, when you achieve professional successes, (i.e., a breakthrough with a difficult pupil, a particularly successful lesson, unsolicited praise and affection from pupils), don't be afraid to congratulate yourself. Spend at least as much time focusing on your strengths and accomplishments as you do on your perceived shortcomings.

With respect to coping with instructional stress, allow yourself time to stop and appreciate your ability to control what happens to you. Let yourself know that you are self-sufficient and can control your own reactions to life's trials and tribulations. Don't be afraid to give yourself credit for any success you experience. Developing self-control and active coping skills is extremely important to your personal efficiency. Let yourself know in any way you can how important your accomplishments in this area are.

QUESTIONS AND RESPONSES

This section of Chapters 2 through 6 is intended to clarify common questions, misconceptions, and confusions that instructors may have about the information presented in the chapter. The questions are based on the author's own experiences in working with preservice and in-service teachers.

1. *Q:* I think many of the ideas for coping with stress discussed in this chapter are really interesting, but it seems to me that they would work only for teachers whose anxiety reactions are reasonably mild —at least, not really severe and disabling.

R: It seems obvious that the more mild one's stress/anxiety reactions, the easier they would be to overcome. This is particularly true because the confidence of the mildly anxious individual in attempting to cope with anxiety will likely exceed that of the severely anxious individual. On the other hand, the severely stressed person may have much more motivation to do something about his or her dysfunctional reactions. Individual differences in these matters are great, and there is no easy way of predicting which anxiety/stress victims will benefit most from self-control coping strategies. One recent finding (Barrios and Shigetomi, 1979) indicates that people who believe that their actions and feelings are internally controlled are more likely to cope successfully than those who believe that their actions and feelings are externally determined. Such findings suggest that individual differences may well have more effect than the level of anxiety/stress per se in determining who will benefit more from stress-coping strategies.

2. *Q:* Professional growth is a popular subject, but I'm a bit confused as to what professional growth means. I can see how a teacher continues to learn new things about teaching as a result of greater classroom experience, but it seems to me that when people talk about professional growth, they mean something more than this.

R: I like your definition of professional growth—increased learning about teaching as a consequence of classroom experience. I think it is very important to recognize that when we talk about growth we really are talking primarily about learning new perspectives, strategies, skills, and information. However, I would extend your definition to include pertinent learning about teaching that arises from sources other than direct classroom experience—e.g., reading, seminars and workshops, structured thinking, writing, and informal interaction with colleagues. Learning that is not directly related to teaching but that affects teaching performance (e.g., learning effective coping strategies for dealing with personal anxieties) also should be included in the concept of professional growth. The reason I particularly like your definition is that you have equated growth with learning. Professional growth is learning to teach more and more effectively on an ongoing, day-to-day basis. This is why it is so important that each teacher or prospective teacher take personal responsibility for his or her own professional growth. Leaving professional growth entirely up to school systems, teachers' organizations, and university courses is the biggest single weakness in many teachers' operational notions about professional growth. Any single input (a course, a workshop, an experience) is likely to be ineffective in promoting professional learning (growth) unless the teacher actively and purposefully engages in continuous elaboration and extension of his or her active instructional repertoire.

3. *Q:* Sometimes I think that the entire business of stress management is overblown. Teaching seems to attract an endless series of "bandwagon" kinds of issues. Isn't this current emphasis on stress just one more example of this?

R: I agree that teaching seems to attract more than its share of "bandwagons." I also think that the current wave of stress-management workshops for teachers probably will come and go, just like many other trends have done. However, I think it is important to realize that success at any job can be heavily influenced by general attitudes and personal ways of coping with job demands. An awareness of these attitudes and personal habits and of the possibilities for channelling them to promote professional success and contentment can be of vital importance. Many successful teachers have been involved in such processes without ever being aware of terms such as *stress management.* What I really want to emphasize is the importance of placing one's vocation and its demands in a perspective that permits continuing professional growth and development. I doubt that ways of accomplishing this will ever be outdated.

4. *Q:* I can see how stress management is important, but if a teacher isn't skilled at teaching, all the stress management techniques in the world won't help. Isn't it true that the best way to reduce your anxiety is to increase your competence at what you do?

R: I couldn't agree with you more. In fact, the remaining chapters of this book are devoted to descriptions of specific instructional behaviors and cognitions that define instructional competence per se. Without this basic competence, teachers probably have good reason to feel anxious or stressed. The intention of this chapter has not been to suggest that specific methods of coping with professional stress should be used to cover up lack of professional competence. Rather, it has presented methods for learning to relax and to reduce stress so as to approach the task of developing and extending professional competence in a positive, enthusiastic manner. In the final analysis, attainment of professional competence is the best deterrent to instructional stress or anxiety.

SUGGESTED ACTIVITIES

The activities section at the end of Chapters 2 through 6 is intended to give the reader ideas about how to practice the teaching skills discussed in the chapter.

1. Since this chapter has been concerned entirely with strategies for coping with stress/anxiety, it seems most appropriate to suggest that readers learn the basic method of stress management (or some effective variation of it) described in the chapter. In developing learning programs for acquiring this strategy, the chapter's basic orientation toward self-control and professional growth may be very useful. The best way to learn such techniques is first to locate in your own behaviors, thoughts, and emotions, specific stress/anxiety responses to known stress factors, instructional or otherwise, and then to attempt to use the coping strategy very carefully and gradually to control your reactions to these situations. Even if you are not currently experiencing any teaching-related stress, learning such coping strategies will enable you to employ them to prevent the occurrence or buildup of professional anxieties should they arise in the future. Preservice teachers are in an excellent position to learn coping strategies to control stress/anxiety reactions associated with initial practicum placements and student teacher supervision procedures.

REFERENCES

Barrios, B.A., and Shigetomi, C.C. 1979. Coping skills training for the management of anxiety: A critical review. *Behavior Therapy* 10: 491–522.

Beck, A. 1976. *Cognitive Therapy and Emotional Disorders.* New York: International Universities Press.

Ellis, A. 1962. *Reason and Emotion in Psychotherapy.* New York: Lyle Stuart.

———. 1975. Rational psychotherapy. In *Counseling Children and Adolescents,* edited by W.M. Walsh. Berkeley, Calif.: McCutchan.

Hiebert, B. 1980. *Self-Relaxation: Learn It, Use It.* Coquitlam, B.C.: Per Man Consultants.

Jacobson, E. 1938. *Progressive Relaxation.* Chicago: University of Chicago Press.

Kanfer, F.H., and Goldstein, A.P. 1980. *Helping People Change: A Textbook of Methods.* New York: Pergamon Press.

Meichenbaum, D. 1977. *Cognitive Behavior Modification: An Integrated Approach.* New York: Plenum Press.

Wolpe, J. 1958. *Psychotherapy by Reciprocal Inhibition.* Stanford: Stanford University Press, 1958.

————, and Lazarus, A.A. 1966. *Behavior Therapy Techniques.* New York: Pergamon Press.

3

Preactive Instruction

Much teacher activity occurs before actual instructional interactions with pupils in the classroom. The model for mastering instruction depicted in Figure 3.1 referred to the skills a teacher employs at this time as *preactive instructional skills.* These skills include (1) establishment of general instructional goals, (2) use of task analysis as a basis for preassessment of student capabilities before actual instruction, and (3) establishment of specific instructional objectives based on the results of the preassessment. Together, these skill areas define a vital yet often neglected dimension of instructional behavior.

Reasons for neglect of the area of preactive instruction are many and varied. Many teachers simply do not comprehend why they should expend a great deal of effort on tedious, time-consuming preparation when the "real" teaching and learning action occurs face-to-face with pupils in the classroom. However, without strong preactive instructional skills, as well as the time and inclination to employ them, it is impossible to discharge the more exciting interactive dimensions of instruction in optimally effective ways. The notion seems almost trite, but it really is impossible to stimulate successful learning without

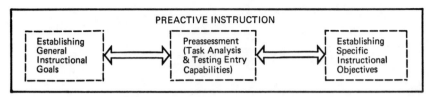

FIGURE 3.1   *The Preactive Phase of Instruction*

knowing what learning is intended to occur and the extent to which each pupil is capable of engaging in specific instructional tasks.

In actual fact, teachers should spend as much time exercising preactive instructional skills as they do engaging in interactive instruction. While working in the preactive area may not be as directly exciting and rewarding as interactive instructional contact, preactive instruction is responsible for much effective pedagogy. Although the time and effort spent in the preactive area is often great when viewed in the short term, it most often results in long-term savings in the teacher's time and energy. Knowing where your instruction is going and how likely it is that your pupils will benefit from it is invaluable information. If used properly, this information can yield substantial returns in both effectiveness, efficiency, and enjoyment. Nothing is more inefficient and frustrating for both teachers and pupils than interactive instruction that is aimless and that takes no account of current pupil capabilities. Being well prepared is a major deterrent to professional stress and anxiety.

There is a great deal of ongoing interplay among the preactive, interactive, and evaluation phases (see Fig. 1.1) during any given lesson. The same is true over a set of lessons that constitute a course or a substantive unit within a given curriculum area. What occurs during any classroom interaction may result in desirable and necessary modifications to the lesson's objectives or preassessments and most certainly influences preactive preparation for the next lesson. Similarly, evaluation of pupil learning and instructional effectiveness during any single lesson will undoubtedly affect both future preactive and interactive strategies. *Instructional planning* should enable the teacher to recognize the practical, ongoing interplay among preactive, interactive, and evaluation skills. A complete plan for each lesson should be based both on careful evaluation of previous classroom instructional interactions (lessons) and on an exacting examination of future instructional goals and objectives. In this sense, one lesson's evaluation can function as a preassessment for future lessons in the curriculum sequence. While all of this "connectedness" may seem a bit difficult to grasp at first, just remember that every phase of instruction must be in harmony with every other phase. It is impossible to consider any aspect of instructional activity without meaningful cross-referencing to other aspects. (Note: Because instructional planning ideally integrates information from preactive, interactive, and evaluation areas, it will be discussed fully in Chapter 6. All the basic skill areas that enter into instructional planning will have been discussed thoroughly at that point.)

Before we turn to an examination of the most basic preactive instructional skill—establishing general instructional goals—it probably would be a good idea if we define the basic terms *instruction* and *learning*. While it is undoubtedly possible to define instruction and learning in many ways, the definitions offered here are derived directly from a consensus of several major viewpoints in the area of instructional psychology (Martin, 1981). *Learning may be taken to refer to any change in an individual's behavioral, cognitive, affective, and/or perceptual repertoire.* As such, a demonstration of learning must involve an enactment of behaviors, cognitions, emotions, or perceptions in contexts where such active processes previously were absent. Given the obvious relations between learning and instruction, *instruction may be defined as any purposeful activity on the part of a teacher that is responsible for changing another person's behavioral, cognitive, affective, and/or perceptual repertoire.* Evidence that instruction has occurred is seen first in the changes in a learner's active repertoire of behaviors, thoughts, emotions, and/or perceptions. It then must be established that these changes have resulted from and are in accord with the instructional actions and objectives that have guided the teacher's interactions with the learner. Notice that, in these definitions, instruction and learning are not limited to knowledge and skills alone, and may include alterations in affect, attitudes, and values. Notice also that the definition of instruction is purposive in that changes in the pupil must be associated with both the actions and the intent of the teacher's instruction. It is quite possible for a pupil to learn many things that the teacher does not intend but that result from the teacher's actions. Consistency throughout instructional purpose, instructional action, and pupil change is necessary before one can say that instruction has occurred. In this sense, instruction is an accountable activity in which teachers are professionally responsible for the learning of their pupils. This is true even though learning actually is demonstrated in the behaviors, thoughts, perceptions, and emotions of the pupils.

ESTABLISHING GENERAL INSTRUCTIONAL GOALS

It is impossible to talk about preactive instructional skills without first considering the general goals of public schooling. Most school systems in North America and most government departments of education subscribe to a formally stated philosophy of education. This is not a typical philosophy in the sense of being a complete, logical treatment of a carefully defined issue or set of issues. Rather, it is a brief statement of what the system or the department is attempting to accomplish on behalf of society and their constituents. Most of these goal statements speak about the development of the individual, both for personal well-being and for the good of society. Philosophies of different local systems place different emphases on the extent to which individual and societal well-being involve maintenance or alteration of current social circumstances and values. Most goal statements compromise these alternatives by expressing the hope that, through schooling, young people will come to understand the past (i.e., cultural heritage) and the present (societal traditions, values, beliefs, attitudes, and practices) so that they may participate competently in the democratic process of contributing to future societal development.

Not surprisingly, educational philosophies in a democratic society are likely to emphasize or be built on strongly democratic values. Tyler (1950) summarizes four common democratic values that are often viewed as basic to an effective and satisfying personal and social life: (1) every individual is an equal human being, regardless of race, nationality, or socioeconomic status; (2) every individual has the opportunity to participate fully in all phases of activity and in all societal groups; (3) individual variations and differences are encouraged, and the rise of a single type of person is not demanded; and (4) individual intelligence, rather than arbitrary autocratic or aristocratic authority, is respected as a factor in solving social problems. When such values are embraced in a school system's operating philosophy, they help to define in very general terms what should be taught and learned during the time a student moves from kindergarten through grade twelve. Thus, instructional goals aimed at imparting knowledge about history, literature, law, morality, and art; developing basic skills in reading, writing, communication, and mathematics; and fostering rational, conceptual, decision-making, and problem-solving abilities can be seen to be in general harmony with the goals of opportunities for self and society. At the very least, broad philosophic considerations may provide an important initial screen that helps to determine what should be taught and learned in the course of public schooling.

In recent decades, a great deal of educational theory has developed around the notion that the most important general goal of public school education should be the development of *self-directed learners*—that is, people who have learned vital strategies for teaching themselves (Coates and Thoresen, 1980). This goal also is in complete harmony with the basic philosophic goals and values of education. Learning how to learn is often viewed as essential to lifelong personal contentment and to social productivity and achievement (Rogers, 1969). The literature suggests that people who control their own learning achieve a level of self-sufficiency and creative initiative that is impossible in the absence of such self-direction.

Broad goals, such as the development of self-directed learners, can act as a screen for the selection of instructional goals in the same sense that broad philosophic statements can. However, in order to be useful to the classroom teacher who must select curriculum materials and learning experiences, instructional goals must be focused on specific grade levels and curriculum areas. Most government education departments now produce curriculum guides and/or statements of instructional goals for each grade level. These statements derive from a breakdown of broad philosophic statements and system goals into more specific instructional goals for the classroom teacher. The process is illustrated in the following example.

Government Philosophy: Hypothetical excerpt from a typical statement regarding education.

> Education is concerned with the development of perspectives, actions, values, and beliefs fundamental to the society that

has established schools for this purpose. It is further concerned with the development of individuals with insight into the past and present and the ability to contribute to the future.

School District Goals: Some goals that may be viewed as being in harmony with the government philosophy.

- Students will develop the ability to understand and communicate ideas and feelings for personal, social, scholastic, business, professional, and vocational purposes.
- Students will develop the skills of acquiring and communicating knowledge.
- Students will cultivate and maintain self-confidence and a sense of self-worth.

Curriculum Area Goals: (Some goals in reading and English) that may be seen as being in harmony with the school district goals.

- Learners will demonstrate positive attitudes about reading by choosing to read a broad range of written material.
- Students will understand that writing has a variety of functions and that each function is associated with a particular writing form, style, and vocabulary.

Grade-Level Goals: Some goals for grade eight that are in line with the curriculum area goals.

- Students will be able to write expository paragraphs.
- Students will write a variety of documents, including outlines, diaries, letters, and records of trips and experiences.
- Students will read from a diverse selection of materials, including poems, novels, legends, magazines, and newspapers.

Notice that each of the instructional goals described is stated in terms of what the learner (student) will learn (understand, be able to do, develop) rather than in terms of what the teacher will do. This is an important point because it emphasizes that instructional goals are concerned primarily with *what* students should learn in the school years, not with *how* a teacher goes about facilitating learning. The initial focus of instruction should always be on the student; in this sense, all instruction is student-centered. Beginning our consideration of specific instructional behaviors by focusing on the establishment of instructional goals from the learner's point of view helps to reinforce this central idea. As we will see later in this chapter (see discussions of preassessment and instructional objectives), this method of stating instructional goals and purposes also helps the teacher determine what the learner must be able to do in order to learn. As a result, the teacher can become more aware of possible learning difficulties and hurdles. These insights in turn are invaluable for the planning and selection of interactive instructional skills and strategies. Whether or not a given government or school system has suggested grade-level and curriculum area instructional goals, each teacher should understand the gradual specification process illustrated in the preceding example. Only by being able to establish instructional goals that take into account societal values and norms can teachers begin to comprehend the relevance of their instruction to their pupils' lifelong learning.

PREASSESSMENT

Preassessment is the process by which a classroom teacher discovers what each pupil knows and can do (as well as what each doesn't know and cannot do) in relation to a particular instructional goal. Preassessment must precede both planning and engaging in interactive instruction aimed at accomplishing the goal. Before preassessment can begin, one or more grade-level and curriculum area goals must be stated in terms of what each learner will be able to do or understand when the instructional goal has been achieved. Once the preassessment has been conducted, the teacher may use this information to determine existing pupil knowledge and skills (capabilities). Such information is invaluable for the establishment of more specific objectives that will help to guide the actual development and implementation of interactive curriculum and instructional strategies.

The basic reason for conducting a preassessment is, quite simply, "to determine where each pupil presently is at" in relation to valid instructional goals. The acquisition and use of good preassessment skills helps the teacher to avoid two of the most common errors of instruction. The first error is the assumption by the teacher that pupils can do and/or know things they really cannot. The second error is the assumption that pupils cannot do and/or know things that they really can. Both errors are likely to result in all kinds of frustration for both teacher and pupils and to waste valuable classroom time. The first error renders effective instruction impossible because the pupils do not possess the necessary *entry capabilities* (i.e., all the things that pupils know and/or can do before interactive instruction occurs) to benefit from the teacher's actions. The second error also prevents effective instruction because the teacher simply reenacts past learning experiences that have already been successful. The pupil frustration (in the former instance) and boredom (in the latter instance) occasioned by these errors can be powerful impediments to positive classroom learning.

The basic skills necessary to perform valid and reliable preassessments so as to avoid errors of either overestimating or underestimating pupil entry capabilities are (1) task analysis and (2) testing entry capabilities.

Task Analysis

Task analysis (Gagné, 1977) is a preactive instructional skill that enables the teacher to recognize many of the crucial understandings and performances that a pupil must be able to employ in order to attain any given instructional goal. Most of the learning tasks contained in any instructional goal can be subdivided into a number of less complex tasks. This process of task reduction often clarifies which pupil capabilities are necessary to accomplish the goal by indicating which capabilities are necessary to accomplish the less complex tasks.

Task analysis involves three sequential steps:

1. *operationalization* of the instructional goal in terms of what pupils must be able to do in order to attain it;

2. *listing* of all the more simple pupil actions and capabilities that are prerequisite or corequisite to performance of the overall instructional task; and
3. *sequencing* of these pupil actions and capabilities in terms of which specific actions are required for the successful performance of which other actions.

To accomplish the first step, the instructor must ask, "What must pupils do in order to demonstrate that they understand the concepts and/or are competent in performing the tasks assumed by the instructional goals?" In order to answer this question, it is necessary to *operationalize* (i.e., make concrete in terms of overall pupil capabilities) the instructional goal itself. Goals that are not stated in terms of pupil understanding and performance must be restated with that emphasis. Thus, an instructional goal stated as, "To teach students about Canadian history" is much less useful for the purposes of task analysis than the same goal stated as, "Students will acquire basic information about important people and events in the history of Canada and will demonstrate their acquisition of such information in a variety of ways (including logical arguments about the causes of major events and the association of key figures with the events in which they were active)." It is always possible to state goals in more and more concrete ways. The basic point is that, unless goals are converted at least partially to statements that address pupil performance, they will be of little use for assessing what pupils must do to attain such goals. Without this information, the teacher has a weak foundation for the planning and execution of classroom instruction and for being aware of difficulties that pupils might experience in their learning endeavors.

The second step in task analysis is to *list* all pupil actions and capabilities that are prerequisite or corequisite to the accomplishment of the overall instructional goal. Two examples of the listing process should help to clarify it. The first example breaks down an instructional goal appropriate for primary grade (early elementary) children. The second example does the same for a typical secondary grade (high school) instructional goal.

EXAMPLE 1
(based on an example in Glaser and Reynolds, 1964):*

Instructional Goal: Students will be able to tell time by writing or saying aloud the time indicated on the clock to an accuracy of one minute.

Listing of Pupil Capabilities:
- Differentiating the little hand from the big hand.
- Reading the number on the clock to which the little hand is pointing.
- Reading the number on the clock that the little hand has just passed.
- Determining the number indicated by the little hand.
- Writing the number of hours indicated by the little hand.
- Writing and reading numbers from 0 to 59.
- Writing "00" when the big hand points to the top center of the clock.
- Associating the word "o'clock" with "00" and the top center of the clock.
- Saying words needed to describe time (e.g., "one-twelve," "o'clock," "after," "before," "to," "of," "quarter," "half," "minutes," "hours").
- Counting clockwise by ones every single mark from the zero point to determine the number indicated by the big hand.
- Counting clockwise by fives every fifth mark from the zero point to determine the number indicated by the big hand.
- Determining the number indicated by the big hand.
- Writing the number of minutes the big hand indicates.
- Associating "minutes after'" with the number indicated by the big hand.
- Associating "hours" with the number indicated by the little hand.
- Associating "minutes after" with the numbers indicated by the big hand when it is off top center.

---

* This example has been modified and included here with the kind permission of the University of Pittsburgh Press.

- First saying the number the minute hand indicates when it is off top center; then saying "minutes after" when the minute hand is off top center; then saying the number the hour hand indicates when the minute hand is off top center.

(This is not a complete list of all the things children must learn to reach the instructional goal; however, it should illustrate the importance of task analysis for clarifying the number and variety of elements in which learners must be instructed in relation to any relatively complex instructional goal. Such knowledge is invaluable to the teacher as a means of diagnosing present or past learning failures, and providing a setting for success in learning.)

EXAMPLE 2

Instructional Goal: Students (grade ten) will write a brief essay (expounding on no more than three central points or arguments) on any topic of their choice.

Listing of Pupil Capabilities:
- Reading and writing a vocabulary appropriate to grade ten level (the exact nature of this vocabulary will be elaborated further).
- Spelling an adequate grade ten vocabulary.
- Applying skills in punctuation and grammatical construction necessary to convey intended meanings.
- Writing a variety of simple and complex sentences.
- Writing basic descriptive, narrative, and expository paragraphs.
- Generating a variety of alternative topics.
- Deciding on a single topic from a variety of alternatives on the basis of personal knowledge, competence, interest, and ability.
- Using library, community, and personal resources to research and collect information concerning a topic.
- Making research notes that can be referred to during the planning and writing of the essay.

- Associating ideas and information in clusters that relate to central arguments or points.
- Organizing topical ideas, thoughts, and major arguments by means of conceptualizing and writing a detailed topical outline.
- Conceptualizing central arguments through logical analysis, comparison and contrast, synthesis and summation.
- Writing a lead paragraph that gives an overview of the central arguments, points, and concepts of the essay.
- Writing body paragraphs that possess an obvious major (topic) sentence and a variety of supporting sentences.
- Writing a concluding paragraph that revisits briefly each central point or argument and expresses an overall conclusion or viewpoint.
- Editing the essay for spelling, punctuation, and grammatical errors.
- Critically editing to ensure that the student has said what he or she intended to say.
- Redrafting portions of the essay to improve logical sequence, flow, impact, and clarity.

The third step in a complete task analysis is to *sequence* all the pupil actions and capabilities generated in the second step. Specific capabilities that are prerequisite to other capabilities should be listed before the latter. Such a logical sequence is extremely important to the second skill required for preassessment of pupil capabilities (testing entry capabilities). With an unorganized list of pupil capabilities such as the one in Example 1, preassessment would take forever. Each separate capability would need to be tested for each pupil in the classroom. To avoid this unnecessary expenditure of time and energy, the teacher can make an educated guess about where most pupils are likely to be in relation to an organized (sequenced) list of prerequisites. Pupil entry capabilities then can be tested in the immediate vicinity of the guess. To facilitate this process (which will be described in more detail in the next section), the third step of a task analysis is preparation of a sequenced list of pupil capabilities relevant to the attainment of an instructional goal. Each capability on this list is preceded by more basic capabilities on which it depends and is succeeded by more complex capabilities to which it contributes.

The list of pupil capabilities in Example 2 was constructed in accordance with my own attempt to produce a sequenced list of the capabilities required for writing a basic essay. Contrasting the logical sequence of prerequisites in Example 2 with the nonsequenced, random list in Example 1 should help to clarify the purpose of the third step of task analysis.

The bases on which pupil capabilities are sequenced may include both logical and empirical-developmental considerations. The kind of analysis that teachers conduct to determine the logical sequence of pupil capabilities is largely a function of each teacher's competence and experience. The more familiarity a teacher has with a particular age group or grade level, the more likely that the analyses of tasks from simple to complex will coincide with the natural development and learning sequences for each pupil's experiences. Nonetheless, it is important to remember that what may seem to a teacher like a relatively simple subtask is not always so simple when viewed from a natural developmental perspective. Most teachers can benefit from supplementing their logical analyses of task sequences with insights from careful empirical observation of children's learning and development. Literature dealing with this area is readily available in a variety of sources (e.g., Lefrancois, 1977).

Testing Entry Capabilities

The second skill required for successful preassessment of pupil entry capabilities is the valid and reliable determination of each pupil's current status in relation to each instructional goal and its task analysis. Sound task analysis sets the stage for the actual *testing of entry capabilities*. If done well, task analysis can safeguard valuable instruction/learning time and ensure efficient individual preassessments. In short, task analysis helps the teacher to determine *what* entry capabilities to preassess; *how* to test for entry capabilities is the subject of this section.

In order to avoid elaborate testing for all the entry capabilities indicated by a thorough task analysis, the teacher can make informed estimates of what prerequisite capabilities pupils are like to have in relation to each instructional goal. This estimate is a rough judgment based both on general knowledge of current and previous grade-level curricula and on the teacher's own experiences with other pupils at similar grade levels. Slight inaccuracy in the estimate is insignificant, since the sole purpose of this initial guess is to minimize the amount of pretesting or preassessment necessary for accurately establishing each pupil's current level of capability.

Once the teacher has made the initial estimate, he or she can begin to test the pupil capabilities that immediately precede and follow the points of the estimate. Through this process, and with some trial and error, the teacher eventually can determine the capability levels at which most of his or her pupils can perform. The teacher also can determine the range of entry capabilities that typify that particular class. Such information will enable each teacher to establish precise instructional objectives for the class as a whole and for individual pupils. Testing for entry capabilities helps to ensure that precise instructional objectives will be attainable and stimulating for each pupil. The process also minimizes the possibility of underestimating or overestimating current levels of pupil ability.

Testing for entry capabilities may be done in a variety of ways, depending on the teacher's determination of the best and most efficient way to obtain valid and reliable information about each pupil. (See Chapter 5 for a detailed discussion of reliability and validity in testing. Although Chapter 5 deals with the evaluation of learning during and after classroom instruction, the same principles apply to preassessment.) The three most common preassessment methods are (1) formal *written* tests (either standardized or composed by the teacher); (2) *oral* questioning and discussion; and (3) precise *observation* of pupils' task activities. Supplementary information from pupil files, previous reports, interviews with previous teachers, and discussions with parents may also be employed. Supplementary information, however, should *never* be used in the absence of these methods. Teachers should always take the time to find out for themselves what each pupil can and cannot do; the reports and opinions of others qualify only as second-hand information. Some of it may be useful, but it also may be colored by perceptions that have little relation to a pupil's academic capabilities per se. Premature labeling of pupils on the basis of external information can lead a teacher unwittingly to provide differential instructional treatment to different pupils (see Rosenthal and Jacobson, 1968).

The decision to use the written, oral, or observational preassessment method or some combination thereof depends largely on the nature of the specific capability being assessed. For example, if the capability in question is "counting clockwise by ones, every single mark from the zero point to determine the number indicated by the big hand," either the written or the oral method could be employed (e.g., writing down the big-hand numbers indicated by a variety of clock faces on a sheet of paper, or calling out the big hand numbers indicated by the teacher equipped with a large instructional clock). For other capabilities, such as "writing a lead paragraph that overviews the central arguments, points, and concepts of a planned essay," a written preassessment asking the pupil to perform the task is clearly indicated. Direct observation of pupil performances is the method of choice when the particular capability involves direct actions, such as manipulating and setting up laboratory equipment, typing, or leading group discussions.

Sometimes it is useful to combine written, oral, and observational methods simply to ensure that preassessment is not biased by the method of testing. Some pupils perform better in oral than in written modalities. Others perform observable activities that indicate skills and knowledge they can't yet talk or write about. This does not suggest that pupils should not learn to perform better in the modalities in which they are weakest. (Indeed, such performance increments should be noted as necessary instructional objectives for specific pupils.) However, from the perspective of preassessment alone, the sole purpose of a teacher's testing efforts is to determine what pupils currently do and don't know, what they can and can't do. In order to get this information, a teacher should give pupils every opportunity to perform in ways that indicate their true abilities.

An important but often overlooked aspect of testing for entry capabilities is the opportunity it provides for teachers to get to know their pupils as separate individuals with unique sets of interests, preferences, and enthusiasms. When preassessing for skills and knowledge, a teacher should never miss the opportunity (whether in a general oral class discussion, an individual interview, or an informal skill-observation situation) for talking to pupils about their interests, likes and dislikes, and aspirations. Such information is often invaluable for selecting and arranging subsequent instructional activities that will be meaningful to pupils. While a teacher's primary task is to assist pupils in the acquisition of new knowledge and skills, this task cannot be accomplished effectively in the absence of affective information that contributes to maximizing pupil motivation and enthusiasm.

ESTABLISHING SPECIFIC INSTRUCTIONAL OBJECTIVES

Once the teacher has established general instructional goals and obtained accurate information concerning each pupil's related capabilities, he or she is in a position to combine these two sets of information to create specific instructional objectives. These objectives guide the actual planning and implementation of interactive instructional skills and strategies. Instructional *objectives* are much more narrow in focus than instructional *goals*. Several specific objectives should guide each classroom lesson. Over time the learnings associated with series of short-term instructional objectives should cumulate into performance and knowledge increments that will serve broader instructional goals. Instructional objectives help to guide the formulation of active instruction. Active instruction takes learners from where they are to where they can demonstrate, both to themselves and to others, the knowledge and skills associated with higher level instructional goals.

In our discussion of instructional goals we initially described the difference between stating goals and objectives from the student's point of view and stating them from the teacher's point of view. Consider the following brief examples.

1. (a) To teach the basic research skills of using null hypotheses and logical alternative hypotheses to clarify research questions.
   (b) The student will be able to formulate and write statements of null hypotheses and logical alternative hypotheses that clarify a variety of research questions.

2. (a) To show students the difference between mammals and reptiles.
   (b) Students will state the essential defining characteristics of mammals and reptiles and will be able to identify correctly instances of each animal class from a variety of examples.

Notice that the student-centered goals in these examples (1b and 2b) focus on what students will be able to do as a result of learning something new. Such statements are very useful for giving the teacher a clear idea of when learning has taken place. Remember that the overall purpose of instruction is to facilitate learning. Thus, before the teacher can determine whether effective instruction has occurred, it is necessary to determine whether the students have learned anything. Student-centered goals and objectives help the teacher to focus first on the essential matter of student learning.

The second major advantage of student-centered goals and objectives is that they subordinate teaching to learning in terms of overall instructional planning. The teacher should begin instructional planning with a precise notion of intended learning outcomes. This allows consideration of a variety of interactive instructional activities, strategies, and curriculum materials that could be used to promote these outcomes. On the other hand, if the teacher begins planning with a rigid notion of his or her instructional intentions, potential variety and the possibility of creatively matching instructional methods to learning tasks will be severely limited. The inflexibility and closed-mindedness that can result from overemphasis on what you will do as a teacher, along with ignorance of what efforts students will devote to learning, is illustrated vividly in the following teacher comment:

> I don't know why so many people find teaching to be so hard. All you have to do is lecture clearly, supervise seat-work practice, and correct errors. What could be simpler. I mean, you just do your job and from there those pupils who can learn will, and those that can't won't! This is simply the reality of teaching.

While this comment indicates an instructional strategy that might be very effective for certain kinds of objectives and learners, it is doubtful that it is equally useful for every purpose and every pupil. If you make sure to think about what learners will be doing when they learn specific things before you consider the ways in which you can help them learn, instruction becomes a much more creative and potentially effective enterprise. Getting locked into a single method of instruction can become a limiting factor with respect to both instructional effectiveness and growth.

We have seen that an instructional goal is a broad statement of intended outcomes for pupil learning. In contrast, *instructional objectives are specific statements of what learners will be able to do during and/or after an instance of instruction that they cannot do before that instruction.* While instructional objectives may be written in many ways, they generally should meet the following criteria (Dick and Carey, 1978; Mager, 1962; Popham and Baker, 1970):

1. Objectives should include a clear statement of what learners will *do* (i.e., how they will behave) to demonstrate that they have learned.
2. Objectives should include a statement of the *conditions* under which pupils will be able to demonstrate learning.
3. Objectives should include a statement of the *criteria* that pupil learning actions must meet or exceed.

Let us consider each of these criteria briefly. The following examples will demonstrate the first criterion by giving illustrations of different objectives stated first in imprecise, nonbehavioral terms, and then in precise, behavioral terms. Notice that the second statement of each objective allows you to imagine exactly what a pupil will be doing if learning occurs. Such statements are invaluable for charting pupil progress and instructional effectiveness.

1. (a) Students *will know* about Freud.
   (b) Students will be able *to state and describe* several key events and persons in Freud's life and *describe* in some detail Freud's theories of motivation, psychosexual development, personality, mental illness, and therapy through psychoanalysis.

2. (a) Students *will enjoy* a field trip in the mountains.
   (b) Students *will make many unsolicited statements* that express their enjoyment during a mountain field trip (e.g., "Oh man, this is too much," "Hey, beautiful!" "Look at the view," etc.)
3. (a) Students *will understand* quadratic equations.
   (b) Students *will solve* quadratic equations of the general form $Ax^2 + Bx + C = 0$.

It should be obvious from these examples that the basic method of transforming imprecise objectives into more precise, and thus more useful, objectives consists of using *action verbs* that specify clearly what a student will do. *Passive verbs* that express the learner's general state, such as understanding, enjoyment, or knowing, are of much less use. Learning to write objectives in terms of specific pupil actions is the most important aspect of using instructional objectives to plan effective instruction.

The second criterion that instructional objectives should meet, though less important than the first, is useful for helping to specify the *conditions* under which student learning actions might reasonably be expected to occur. Consider the following restatements of some of the objectives presented in previous examples.

1. *Given five quadratic equations of the general form $Ax^2 + Bx + C = 0$,* students will be able to solve them *without the aid of notes or texts.*
2. *Without any prompting or external pressure to do so,* students will express their enjoyment of a mountain field trip through statements such as "Oh man, this is too much," "Hey, beautiful," "Look at that view," and the like.
3. *Given several general research questions,* students will be able to formulate relevant null hypotheses and logical alternative hypotheses that clarify the research questions.

The italicized portions of these objective statements can help the teacher determine the situations in which demonstrations of pupil learning will occur. This information also can assist the teacher in conceptualizing reasonable evaluation strategies for testing changes in learning. By clarifying the specific cirumstances that surround demonstrations of learning, teachers can help pupils to understand exactly what is expected of them.

The third criterion for writing useful instructional objectives also can help pupils to understand what levels of performance are expected of them and can assist teachers in evaluating both learning and teaching effectiveness. The italicized portions of the following objectives indicate statements of performance (learning) criteria for individual students and/or a group of students.

1. Given five quadratic equations of the general form $Ax^2 + Bx + C = 0$, *all* students will be able to solve correctly *at least* three of the five equations without the aid of notes or texts.
2. Given four different research questions, *at least 70 percent of the students in the class* will be able to formulate relevant null hypotheses and logical alternative hypotheses to clarify *all four* research questions.
3. Given a number of cutout triangles and circles of different shapes, sizes, and colors, children will be able to sort the triangles and circles into two category piles with *90 percent accuracy.*

Notice that, when all three criteria for writing instructional objectives are combined, the intended learning outcomes become clear and specific. Writing a few specific instructional objectives for each lesson or active instructional session is an excellent way of discovering how you, as a teacher, will know whether the intended learnings occur. Communicating such information to your pupils at the beginning of interactive instruction helps them to understand what the class is about, what is expected of them, and what they can do to assist in their own learning.

There are many options, of course, that can be incorporated into the statement and use of specific instructional objectives. Objectives may be primarily *cognitive* (related to how pupils demonstrate thinking skills), *affective* (related to how pupils demonstrate changes in affect or emotion), or *psychomotor* (related to overt movements and actions). They may be *short term* (for a single lesson) or *long term* (for an entire unit or course). At times they may be *process oriented* as much as *product oriented* (e.g., "Students will discuss rationally, and in a manner that demonstrates respect for and understanding of, their own and others' views on national unity issues"). Process-oriented objectives are very specific about skills that are used to carry out an activity but are not concerned particularly with an exact measurable outcome of the activity per se. Process-oriented objectives are extremely important for the teaching of values clarification, thinking, and interpersonal strategies.

Generally speaking, it is more difficult to state specific instructional objectives for affective and high-level cognitive learning outcomes than it is for psychomotor and low-level outcomes. While the latter are more easily stated, the former are just as important (if not more so, depending on the pupils' level of development). With practice you can learn to use specific language for very complex learning tasks (e.g., "Students will compare and contrast the contributions of Shakespeare and Marlowe, discuss the sociological factors that influenced both playwrights, and, through this analysis, generate a theory of the ways in which a writer's social situation can influence his or her work."). It is very important that teachers learn to use objectives for complex as well as simple learning outcomes. Focusing exclusively on simple outcomes because they can be stated more easily is really an abuse of the preactive skill of establishing instructional objectives.

Taken together, employing preactive instructional skills (establishing general goals, performing preassessments, and establishing specific objectives) sets the stage for effective interactive instruction. Because practice of these skills increases the likelihood that classroom instruction will run smoothly and efficiently, they can have a salutary effect on professional stress and anxiety. Teachers who are well prepared (i.e., who know their precise direction) are able to control their instructional energies and reactions in ways that enhance their professional well-being.

QUESTIONS AND RESPONSES

1. *Q:* I can see how instructional objectives can help students know what's expected of them and can help teachers evaluate whether they have been successful in promoting learning. Nonetheless, it seems to me that always telling students what to do is pretty authoritarian. I don't really want to come across as a fascist dictator.

   R: Remember first of all that the sole purpose of instruction is to help learners learn. If objectives help a teacher to do this, then the objectives are serving their purpose. Remember, too, that you can use objectives in many ways. All teachers have some idea about what is going to occur in each lesson. A statement of objectives to the students simply lets the students know as well. In this sense, students can be honestly and openly involved in and knowledgeable about instructional activities and purposes. Most important, there is no reason at all why teachers should not involve their pupils in discussions of general instructional goals and solicit their assistance in determining specific objectives. Such discussions can be held once a week (e.g., on Monday mornings), or at the end of each lesson so as to plan the next instructional period in that curriculum area. Even very young children can get involved in such processes as long as the teacher uses language appropriate to their learning levels. Sharing of instructional preparation helps teach students both to plan their own learning and gradually to take more and more responsibility for self-education. This sharing and the process of interaction surrounding it can help the teacher to become more relaxed and open in interactions with pupils. This in turn can reduce stress associated with lack of communication in the classroom.

2. *Q.:* I can see that establishing goals, doing presassessments, and establishing specific instructional objectives could help to ensure more effective instruction. But to do all these things really takes a lot of time. I can't see myself spending two hours preparing for each hour of class time—that's a twenty-four-hour job!

R: I really can identify with that concern. It does take a lot of time and energy to practice these preactive instructional skills well. On the other hand, I think that the first few times you do this kind of preparation may be misleading. In the first place, like any other skill, preactitve skills become more refined with use. What takes you two hours now will take you a half hour after a month's practice. The second point to keep in mind is that there is a great deal of overlap among different goals. If you do a really good, thorough task analysis for an important goal in the area of, say, language arts and follow it up with detailed testing of relevant entry capabilities, many parts of this preassessment will apply to instructional goals in other aspects of language arts. If you keep careful records of what students can and cannot do in relation to major goals and to each day's lessons, that information will suffice as preassessment information for many future goals. Learning both to make single preassessments serve multiple goals and to integrate preassessment testing into ongoing lesson activities really can minimize the time you spend doing these things. Finally, remember that, without the information that good preassessments can provide, it is likely that you will waste much class time teaching pupils what they already know, or continuously backtracking because you find that students don't know what you thought they knew. Such situations can be frustrating and stressful for both teacher and pupils.

3. *Q:* I'm concerned that the emphasis on setting goals and objectives takes away opportunities for affective, creative spontaneity in the class periods themselves.

R: I think many of us have felt this concern at one time or another. The important thing to realize is that you should not try to do too much in any one lesson. Trying to work around one, two, or three specific objectives is more than enough for a single period. Always plan to include some "flex-time" so that when exciting, unplanned things occur (and you interpret them as beneficial for the overall growth and development of your pupils), you can allow them to continue. The establishment of objectives based on good preassessments helps to ensure that lesson time will be used efficiently for at least some relevant pupil learning. Such preactive techniques should not pretend to "corner the market" on what is permissible and what is not. When unscheduled events occur that can increase pupil interest in general classroom proceedings and that can further a positive learning environment, make the most of them. Instructional planning should always be flexible enough to encompass several alternative activity patterns. There are many ways of reaching an objective. This is why it is a good idea to start planning from the viewpoint of what the learner learns rather than what the teacher teaches.

4. *Q:* I still don't see the difference between a task analysis and an instructional objective.

R: Task analysis is the breaking down of a complex, general goal into a series of subtasks so as to recognize what capabilities (skills and knowledge) pupils must have to accomplish the goal. An instructional objective is a more precise and complete statement (including conditions and criteria) of what pupils will be able to do when they acquire relevant capabilities. While there may be a one-to-one correspondence between each subtask and a specific instructional objective, it is important to remember that task analysis is a means of *identifying* relevant pupil learning actions, while an instructional objective is a *statement* of learning actions in a complete, purposive manner that will guide interactive instruction.

SUGGESTED ACTIVITIES

1. Determine one or two general instructional goals for the grade level and curriculum area you presently teach or hope to teach. Provide a philosophical and practical rationale for your goal selections. Why are these goals important to the individual and/or to society?

2. Do a detailed task analysis of one of the goals you stated in activity one. Include the steps of (a) goal operationalization, (b) listing of pupil capabilities, and (c) sequencing of pupil capabilities. Also discuss how you would test for pupil entry capabilities. What testing methods would be appropriate?

3. Guess at which level on your sequenced task analysis your current or anticipated pupils will be. Write specific instructional objectives with respect to the pupil learning capabilities indicated by this level and the ones immediately surrounding it. Try to write at least one objective each in the cognitive, affective, and psychomotor domains. Do your objectives use action verbs? Do they state conditions and criteria?

REFERENCES

Coates, T.J., and Thoresen, C.E. 1980. Behavioral self-control and educational practice: Do we really need self-control? *Review of Research in Education* 1980: 3–45.

Dick, W., and Carey, L. 1978. *The Systematic Design of Instruction.* Glenview, Ill.: Scott, Foresman and Co.

Gagné, R.M. 1977. *Conditions of Learning.* 3d ed. New York: Holt, Rinehart and Winston.

Glaser, R, and Reynolds, J.H. 1964. "Instructional objectives and programmed instruction: A case study." In *Defining Educational Objectives,* edited by C.M. Lindvall. Pittsburgh: University of Pittsburgh Press.

Lefrancois, G.R. 1977. *Of Children.* Belmont, Calif.: Wadsworth.

Mager, R.F. 1962. *Preparing Instructional Objectives.* Belmont, Calif.: Fearon.

Martin, J. 1981. *Instruction Is Prescriptive.* Paper presented at the Annual Meeting of the Canadian Educational Research Association, Halifax, Nova Scotia.

Popham, W.J., and Baker, E.L. 1970. *Systematic Instruction.* Englewood Cliffs, N.J.: Prentice-Hall.

Rogers, C. 1969: *Freedom to Learn.* Columbus, Ohio: Charles E. Merrill.

Rosenthal, R., and Jacobson, L. 1968. *Pygmalion in the Classroom.* New York: Holt, Rinehart and Winston.

Tyler, R. 1950. *Basic Principles of Curriculum and Instruction.* Chicago: University of Chicago Press.

4

Interactive Instruction

Preactive instructional behaviors set the stage for effective consideration and enactment of interactive instructional behaviors. Once a
teacher has determined systematically (with the use of instructional
goals, preassessments, and specific instructional objectives) exactly
what learners can do and what they should be able to do as a result
of effective instruction, it is time for that teacher to consider exactly
what to do to facilitate desirable pupil learning. Notice once again
that questions of what to teach and how to teach it should always
follow questions of what pupils need to learn. In this chapter we will
consider how a teacher can present instructional curricula that make
appropriate use of known learning principles. This discussion will be
followed by a detailed examination of a teacher's in-class behavior—
that is, the specific instructional skills and strategies that a teacher can
use to promote efficient learning. While most readers probably will
find the material in this chapter more interesting than the material in
the previous chapter, it should always be remembered that interactive
instruction cannot be considered without a firm understanding of
intended learning outcomes and current pupil capabilities. This is so

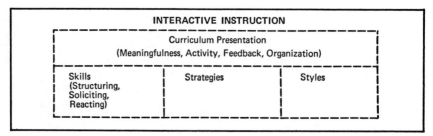

FIGURE 4.1   *The Interactive Phase of Instruction*

because the selection of interactive behaviors is *purposive*. Different interactive skills can have entirely different instructional/learning effects. Knowledge of your direction logically precedes the expenditure of effort to get there.

CURRICULUM PRESENTATION

Curriculum presentation refers to the ways in which teachers arrange and present instructional activities or courses of study. There is no one way to present curriculum. Modes of presentation should vary in accordance with different instructional objectives. Nonetheless, it is possible to identify certain key learning principles, which should be incorporated into almost any type of curriculum presentation. These learning principles may be referred to as (1) meaningfulness, (2) activity (practice), (3) feedback, and (4) organization.

Meaningfulness

Pupils learn more readily when the instructional curriculum is meaningful to them (Underwood and Swartz, 1960). Meaningfulness refers to the number and quality of associations or connections that learners can make between what they will learn and what they already know. Thus, meaningfulness is a very personal and individual matter. The problem that often occurs in instruction is that the teacher's associational networks are likely to be very different from those of students. Thus, while a teacher may attach meaning to a mathematics curriculum through an association of mathematics with daily budgeting, shopping, and survival, grade three pupils may be incapable of drawing similar associations. Consequently, the meaning or relevance of the curriculum may escape them entirely. It becomes the teacher's job to assist pupils in making associations between what they already know through their own experiences and what they will learn in the classroom. This is how a teacher makes curriculum meaningful.

There are many ways to inject meaning into instructional curriculum presentations. The basic strategy always should be to keep pupils completely informed about (and, hopefully, involved in the formulation of) instructional goals and objectives. Students always should know what they are trying to learn. If goals are complex, it is the teacher's responsibility to translate them into language that pupils can comprehend readily. Once pupils understand what they are attempting to learn, the teacher should explain clearly what he or she will do to help them learn. There should be no secrets about teaching/learning exchanges. All participants should understand the rules of the game and communication should be open. If the teacher asks certain kinds of questions, he or she should let the students know that the questions are meant to help students learn, not to catch them off guard, ridicule them, or make fun of them. It is the ongoing responsibility of the teacher to ensure both that learners know what he or she is trying to do and that communication channels are not crossed.

Another very useful way of attaching meaning to curriculum presentation is to relate instructional activities and content purposefully to what students already know. Teachers can make a variety of instructional linkages to students' extracurricular experiences, special interests, previous classroom learning, other subjects, and aspirations. Taking the time to relate today's instructional content to what students learned yesterday and what they will learn tomorrow can help them draw such associations for themselves. When past or present experiences and interests of students provide a basis for learning, the teacher should try to incorporate such experiences and interests into classroom interactions. For instance, a discussion of aerodynamic principles can be related to the movements of footballs and basketballs through the air. Physical wave patterns can be related to the movements and properties of stringed instruments. Life cycles of animals can be related to the tadpoles in the swamp behind the school. The importance of sharing and cooperation can be demonstrated by examples of young-sters assisting their parents with younger siblings.

When linking experiences and interests verbally to classroom instruction is not possible because there is too much heterogeneity in pupil backgrounds, teachers can provide in-class demonstrations, role plays, show-and-tell sessions, and models. These methods can help to provide a common experiential base to which new learnings can be attached and associated. For example, students can observe the prop-erties of molds directly by growing mold cultures in the classroom. Cultural artifacts can be circulated among students during relevant social studies classes. Trajectories can be displayed by having volun-teers at the front of the class perform different throwing and dropping actions while walking or running.

Anything a teacher can do to make use of existing pupil experien-tial and knowledge structures or to provide new, shared experiences that relate to ongoing classroom learning can give meaning to class-room proceedings. When curriculum presentation is meaningful, pupils will learn more quickly and will forget less quickly.

Activity

The second principle of learning that teachers should integrate into curriculum presentation is that *active learners who engage in practice appropriate to instructional goals and objectives learn more than passive learners.* In short, if you want students to learn to do some-thing, you must arrange opportunities for them to practice doing whatever is indicated by the instructional objective. For example, if students are attempting to learn how to conduct scientific investiga-tions, they must be given an actual opportunity to conduct one or to experience a simulated sequence of laboratory activities that is re-lated closely to the scientific investigatory process. If learners are to solve quadratic equations, they must be given a chance to practice solving them.

Of course, activity simply for the sake of activity is not neces-sarily related to appropriate practice of the actions indicated by instructional objectives. Pupils may be very active, but their activity may be unrelated or spuriously related to learning tasks. For instance, a field trip to the mountains may be an excellent way to promote meaningful activity for learning about mountain conditions, vegetation, and wildlife; however, if a detailed natural exploration of these phenomena is replaced entirely by a boisterous, backslapping social event, the field trip probably will not provide practice appropriate to the original objective. Active learning is an advantage only when the practice it provides is legitimately related to reasonable instructional goals and objectives.

Remember, too, that lack of physical activity does not always imply mental or cognitive passivity. Students can sit passively in lectures but engage in covert questioning, specialized notetaking, and memory-recall strategies that cognitively are very active. The bottom line with respect to pupil activity is that teachers must know what kinds of pupil actions are important for what kinds of learning. Knowing this, teachers must make every effort to describe and specify these actions to pupils and to promote practice of them.

Feedback

The beauty of activity is that it leads to the enactment of the third important learning principle: *precise informational and motivational feedback helps pupils learn.* Curriculum presentation should be constructed so as to provide ample opportunity for instructional feedback. Feedback to students about their activity and practice can take many forms, some of which are associated more consistently with positive, efficient learning than are others. Feedback may be automatic or supplied, immediate or remote, descriptive or nondescriptive, positive or negative, encouraging or valuing. It may promote both external or internal evaluation and orientations and motivations toward success or failure. Since feedback can appear in so many forms, and because it has such a profound effect on students' motivation to learn, it is an extremely important and complex learning principle.

Generally speaking, *immediate, automatic* feedback is superior to supplied, remote feedback (Axelrod, 1977). If the teacher can arrange opportunities for students to engage in realistic, appropriate practice activities, feedback generally will be both immediate and automatic. For example, for a young boy learning to swing a baseball bat in a modified game situation, an effective swing will result in the immediate and natural (automatic) feedback of the bat hitting the ball and the ball sailing through the air. While all instructional activities cannot be expected to have automatic, natural consequences in the classroom, the more immediate the feedback, the better. It does little good to show pupils how to correct an error in addition a day (or even ten minutes) after they have made the error. The rule of thumb here is, "Nice and quick does the trick; to delay doesn't pay."

Descriptive feedback lets pupils know what they have done and how their actions relate to learning outcomes. Descriptive feedback generally is superior to nondescriptive feedback for promoting learning (Becker, Englemann, and Thomas, 1971). "You were very careful to do all the calculations inside the brackets before doing the calculations outside the brackets, and as a result you got the right answer. You really seem to understand the brackets rule" is a much superior type of feedback to "Hey, great, that's right." (Remember, of course, that even nondescriptive feedback is better than none.)

Positive feedback generally is more useful than negative feedback (Thoresen, 1973). It usually is better to provide immediate descriptive feedback whenever a pupil's learning performances show any sign of improvement than it is to point out every single mistake. By encouraging correct student responses, incorrect responses will become much less frequent. This is true particularly if you include in the positive feedback statement a description of what the learner did correctly.

Feedback should *encourage* learning performances rather than value them (Dinkmeyer and Dreikurs, 1963). Descriptive feedback helps to encourage learning in that it is linked clearly to what the learner has done. Nondescriptive feedback is often associated more with pupils' entire being (particularly in the perceptions of the student) than with pupils' learning actions. To value pupils' actions by saying "Good," "Wonderful," or "Marvelous" without describing what they have done can give the pupil the impression that *they* are "good" or "marvelous" only when they behave in certain ways, and that otherwise they are "bad" or "rotten." It is extremely important that you give feedback clearly about what the pupil *does* rather than what the pupil *is*, and that you help each pupil to perceive and understand this difference. Although you may like or dislike certain pupil actions in relation to instructional purposes, you should always value each child as a unique individual with potential for learning.

When feedback about pupil learning performances is immediate and descriptive, it helps pupils know why what they have done is correct, useful, and important. This information gradually will assist learners in developing their own internal systems of evaluation. Without knowing the relationships between actions and their consequences, students have no basis for developing self-evaluation skills. Immediate, descriptive feedback helps supply such information to the student (Martin and Walsh, 1979).

Finally, positive, descriptive feedback that is contingent on pupil successes helps to build student self-esteem and to promote orientations and motivations toward success. Pupils learn to view themselves more as learners who can be successful than as learners who always will fail (Becker, Englemann, and Thomas, 1971).

Organization

The final learning principle that must be considered carefully in curriculum presentation is that of *organization.* Lessons should be presented so that students receive all information and skills they need to assimilate and accommodate each new bit of knowledge and each new instructional event. A teacher can help to ensure such organization by analyzing all of the learning tasks contained in a given lesson and sequencing their presentation according to current student capabilities and task prerequisites. Many of the skills teachers need in order to organize curriculum presentation in this fashion have been discussed already (see Chapter 3). If you develop a good system for doing initial and ongoing preassessments, you will find it relatively easy to organize curriculum presentations. Good curriculum organization usually involves the sequencing of series of small subtasks so that students will meet with success at every step in the process of learning larger, complex tasks and concepts.

INSTRUCTIONAL SKILLS

Once the teacher has determined the necessity of incorporating principles of learning (meaningfulness, activity, feedback, and organization) into curriculum presentations, he or she must determine which interactive instructional skills can be used to implement these principles in the classroom. That is, what exactly can a teacher do to achieve meaningfulness, feedback, appropriate activity, and organization? How can he or she ensure that pupils will perceive meaningfulness and organization in the intended ways? The answer to such questions lies in a teacher's effective use of interactive instructional skills.

The totality of a teacher's classroom behavior can be defined by three terms: *skills, strategies, and styles. Instructional skills* are relatively short-lived, discrete aspects of teaching behavior that can be described, practiced, and acquired by almost any teacher. As such, they make up the basic repertoire of the professional educator. Just as the tennis player possesses a variety of discrete tennis skills (e.g, forehand groundstroke, backhand, volley, lob, serve), so the teacher can possess a variety of discrete instructional skills, such as asking factual questions, praising pupil responses descriptively, stating objectives, and summarizing class discussions. Later in this section, a wide variety of instructional skills will be defined, classified, and illustrated.

Instructional strategies are sequences or combinations of several teaching skills that can be used for a variety of instructional purposes. Strategies are purposeful arrangements of skills. The tennis player, faced with a strong volleying opponent, may adopt a strategy that consists of hard, deep serves, deep groundstrokes, lobs, and passing shots for the purpose of keeping the opponent from the net. In similar fashion, a teacher who wants to teach factual-recall materal in biology might combine the skills of asking factual questions, providing informational feedback, and structuring repeated practice into an effective strategy for factual instruction. In order to assist pupils in formulating opinions about an important current event, the same teacher may employ a discussion strategy consisting of asking open-ended questions, redirecting one pupil's statements to those of another, and reflecting and probing pupil comments. The important thing to realize is that countless numbers of instructional strategies may be arranged that are appropriate to an equally large and diverse number of instructional objectives. The purpose of strategies is to attain instructional objectives. In short, skills and strategies describe what the teacher does in order to help pupils learn the knowledge and skills contained in instructional objectives. Later in this chapter, a number of frequently employed instructional strategies will be described and illustrated.

Instructional styles add the important, personal stamp of each teacher to the skilled performances described by instructional skills and strategies. An instructional style might best be defined as the sum total of all the characteristics, mannerisms, and personal qualities of an individual teacher that are communicated in a variety of subtle ways to pupils in a classroom. While instructional styles can be altered with a great deal of time and sustained effort, they are not acquired as easily as skills and strategies. In a sense, although teachers can learn all kinds of skills and strategies, they must learn to accept and live with their personal style. While styles can be affected by the acquisition and incorporation of new skills and strategies, it nonetheless is true that stylistic variables color the manner in which each teacher uses specific skills and strategies. Some of the more common elements of teaching style are conveyed by descriptive adjectives like "laissez-faire," "democratic," "authoritarian," "enthusiastic," "warm," "sensitive," and "detached." In order to be more effective, individual teachers must learn to recognize and be aware of their own personal styles. The ultimate goal is to be able to choose and use instructional skills and strategies that are congruent (i.e., in harmony) with individual teaching styles. Appropriate matching of skills and strategies to instructional styles is an important aspect of effective pedagogy.

There are three major categories of instructional skills within which almost all interactive skills can be considered: *structuring, soliciting,* and *reacting* (see Bellack, Kleibard, Hyman, and Smith, 1966). These three skill areas reflect the "bare bones" reality that all forms of instruction involve the arrangement of a learning environment (structuring); the provision of opportunities for pupil involvement or activity (soliciting); and the provision of feedback or instructional responses to pupil involvement (reacting). In short, teachers instruct by structuring, soliciting, and reacting. Not surprisingly, there is a natural one-to-one correspondence between these general skills and the basic principles of learning described earlier (see section on curriculum presentation). That is, structuring skills are interactive means by

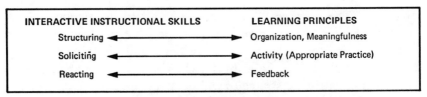

FIGURE 4.2   *Instructional Skills Related to Learning Principles*

which a teacher organizes lesson activities and makes them meaningful for pupils. Soliciting skills are interactive means by which a teacher provides the opportunities essential for pupil activity. Finally, reacting skills provide the all-important ingredient of instructional feedback (Fig. 4.2). *Interactive instructional skills are the vehicles for incorporating important learning principles into ongoing curriculum presentations.*

The following few pages contain a brief taxonomy of structuring, soliciting, and reacting skills. This taxonomy is derived largely from Winne and Martin (1979) (supplemented by Borg, 1973, and Kounin, 1977) and is intended to provide the reader with a ready reference to a variety of commonly employed instructional skills. Such a taxonomy can be invaluable to both preservice and practicing teachers for learning to describe and observe their own classroom behaviors. It also provides basic specifications and illustrations that can assist teachers in experimenting with (and perhaps acquiring) new instructional skills.

Taxonomy of Instructional Skills*

Structuring Skills

Overview

A short presentation at the beginning of a lesson which outlines the major topics to be dealt with and how they will be considered. It may be oral; written on a handout, a chalkboard, a transparency; or a combination of these. A permanent medium, like a handout, can be kept by students for reference.

> "O.K., we're going to look at three major features of a capitalist market economy today: supply, demand, and market equilib-

* The author is indebted to Philip H. Winne for his kind permission to make free use of his contributions to this taxonomy of instructional skills

rium. What do you say to doing this by role playing buyers and sellers? After we get a feel for the way the marketplace works, I'll pose some problem situations and you'll predict how the market would react. . . ."

Statement of Objectives

Clearly stating what students should be able to do after the lesson that they couldn't do before the lesson. The focus may be on goals such as acquiring information, being able to copy a process, applying a strategy, and so on. The communication of objectives may be oral; by a temporary medium, like a chalkboard; or by a permanent medium, like a handout.

> "Goals for today:
> 1. To learn the names and definitions of five characteristics for identifying minerals: color, luster, streak, hardness, and cleavage.
> 2. To identify minerals on the basis of cleavage."

Statement of Curriculum Links

Clearly stating the ways in which information in the current lesson builds on information of past lessons or will form the foundation for future lessons.

> "Last Tuesday, we saw how matter was continuously cycled through an ecosystem via food chains and food webs. Today, we'll make use of the concepts of food chain and food web to examine the flow of energy in a ecosystem."

Topic Summarization within a Lesson

Briefly reviewing the major concepts and their interrelationships that have been presented as part of one of the topics examined in a lesson. Summarization occurs immediately after the topic is finished.

> "O.K., we can see that multiplication is really a special case of addition. When we add, we move along the number line to the right in distances measured unit by unit. When we multiply, we move along the number line to the right in distances measured by groups of units. But if we wanted to, we could break up the groups of units that we use in multiplying into the unit distances we use in adding."

Lesson Review

Briefly reviewing the major topics and their interrelationships that have been presented in the lesson. Review occurs at the end of the lesson.

> "We investigated three major aspects of the physical concept of momentum today. First, we saw that momentum was a characteristic of an object that is defined as the product of its mass and its velocity. Second, we saw that momentum can be transferred from one object to another by contact. And third, we showed that any transfer of momentum results in a transfer of energy between the two objects."

Providing a Model for Student Self-Evaluation of Work

Naming and describing the categories of an answer to questions or exercises that make up a complete response to the learning task, and providing a criterion for each category so that students can compare their responses with a criterion.

> "Now make sure that each answer about urbanization includes something about industrial growth, population influx, and the scarcity of land. Use the definitions of these concepts that we developed yesterday to judge the adequacy of your discussion of each concept as it relates to urbanization."

Verbal Markers of Importance

Using a word or phrase to stress the significance of a fact, a concept, or a process.

> "Now don't forget that it is *absolutely critical* to avoid using ambiguous words like 'sometimes,' 'usually,' 'generally,' or 'probably' when you are trying to be perfectly clear in your compositions."

Statement of Transition

Alerting students to a change in the focus of the lesson's content or process by saying that what was happening is now over and identifying what will occur next.

> "Now that I've finished my little introduction about what we'll do today, let's break up into small groups to begin listing the major concerns of a newly developing nation."

Inducing Set or Providing a Common Basis for Consideration
Presenting an example from common knowledge, a film, a newspaper excerpt, or some other experience that is basically the same for all students as a focus for the lesson or a topic within it.

> "Now I'm sure you've all seen pictures of cracks in the earth that appear during major earthquakes. Let's consider what the crack might look like 5 feet, 100 feet, and one mile below the surface crack that you can see."

Focusing by Rhetorical Question
Asking a question for which you do not expect a student response in order to highlight a significant aspect of the lesson. These questions usually are embedded within a lecture or statement.

> "So we can see that folk songs generally serve to please the listener by providing soothing melodies. But can we also see another important function of the folk song in its lyrics? Yes, because the contemporary folk artist also uses the medium of music for stinging social or political comment."

Physical Arrangement
Placing students and materials in a spatial arrangement that allows, and perhaps encourages, a particular kind of communication.

> Arranging furniture so that students who will share and discuss resource materials are in groups of three to five and face each other in a conversational setting.

Group Alerting Cues
Anything a teacher does to let current nonperformers know that they might be called on.

> "Now, I want everyone to think about this because I might ask any one of you to give the answer."

> "Be thinking of other ways to do this. You may get your chance after Terry has finished."

Soliciting Skills

Fact Recall Questions

Questions that call for the description of a single fact that needs to be aired and incorporated into the consideration of current content.

> "How many electrons are available for bonding in the last column of elements in the periodic table?"

Conceptual Questions

Questions that require the student to manipulate cognitively two or more specific facts to produce an answer. Manipulations may include noting similarities and differences, breaking a whole into component parts, forming a whole from parts, describing the application of a general principle to a specific situation, and so on.

> "What are the basc similarities and differences between the political organization of the U.S.S.R and China?"

Opining or Valuing Questions

Questions that invite students to describe their own opinion about a topic and to describe the foundations underlying that opinion.

> "Jennie, do you think that Tolkien's trilogy *Lord of the Rings* was a good story? What makes you feel that way?"

Judgmental Questions

Questions that require students to determine whether a specific instance does or does not belong to a category of possibilities and to specify the criteria with which they made their classification.

> "Why do you think that Keats was a romantic poet? On what did you base your evaluation?"

Pace

Controlling the speed with which information is brought into the lesson by asking fewer or more questions within a given time span.

Redirecting

Asking the same question of two or more students in succession. Usually, this questioning strategy is used to get a good deal of information into the lesson for consideration later.

> "Nancy, why did the solution change color?"
> "Bill, what's your explanation?"

Prompting Question

A question that follows an incomplete or incorrect student response and that asks the student to justify or elaborate on the first answer. This approach is intended to assist the student in forming the second response by providing a hint or clue about the desired complete response.

> "So you're saying that trade and a country's economic well-being are related, but how does that fit with the idea of the *balance* of trade?"

Probing Question

A question that follows an incomplete or incorrect student response and that asks the student to justify or elaborate on the first answer.

> "Well, Bill, can you tell me a bit more about currents and their effect on temperature?"

Random Recitation Method (RRM)

The teacher calls on pupils (reciters) at random rather than by a predetermined sequence. This prevents pupils from "turning off" when it is "safe" and prevents anxious pupils from getting more and more upset as their turn approaches. RRM keeps all pupils on their toes.

Positive Questioning

The teacher poses a question, pauses for three to five seconds, and then calls upon a reciter. This helps to ensure that all pupils will think about the question.

> "So, what do you think? (Pause) Jimmy?"

Goal-Directed Prompts

The teacher asks questions that focus pupils' attention on their goals by asking them about work plans and/or progress.

> "Now, what is the first step, Sally?"
> "Remember, you've done this before. What was the problem-solving plan you used then?"
> "First of all, you must decide what it is you wish to do."

Showing Work (Calling for Demonstration)

The teacher holds pupils responsible for their work by having them show work or demonstrate skills or knowledge.

> "Susan, come up to the board and let's see how you tackled this problem."
> "I'd like you to tell the rest of the class what your library research revealed."

Promoting Peer Involvement

A kind of redirection in which the teacher involves pupils in the work of their peers by having them respond to each other's recitation or work activity.

> "O.K., Hal, what did you think of Teresa's answer? Can you add anything to it?"
> "Joe's point seems to me to be a bit at odds with something you were saying earlier, Kevin. Do you see any inconsistencies in your positions?"

Reacting Skills

Descriptive Praise

Expressing that a student's response was a good one in a way that emphasizes the connection between the praise comment and the pupil's learning actions.

> "Jamie, that answer was *fabulous*—you really made it clear how oxidation-reduction reactions and energy were related!"

Informational Feedback

Stating the degree to which a student initiation or response is accurate and complete.

> "Well, Jill, the part of your answer that dealt with the role of waterways in national expansion was perfect, but you weren't correct when you described the importance of water transportation relative to the railroad system in the 1890s."

Informational Feedback with Justification

Stating the degree to which a student initiation or response is accurate and complete, and stating a reason as to why that statement was made.

> "That was a beautiful and complete answer, Tom, because you made it perfectly clear how the rhythm of the lines gives you the feeling of the train clickety-clacking over the rails."

Incorporating Student Response into the Lesson

Using a student response explicitly in developing the content or process of the lesson by stating the relevance of the response, acting on its content, or physically incorporating it by putting it on the chalkboard (or other medium) for further use.

> "Let's take your suggestion about the way to regroup the terms within the brackets and factoring out the X^2 terms to see where it leads, Paula."

Post-Response Wait Time

Pausing three or more seconds after a student finishes a statement before engaging in any other teaching act.

"With it" Desists

Telling pupils to stop deviant, off-task behaviors in ways that are timely (administered before the deviant behavior spreads or intensifies), and on target (directed at the pupil who initiated the deviant behavior).

Suggest Alternative Behavior
Diverting the attention of a disruptive pupil to an alternative behavior.

> "O.K., Bill, instead of getting angry, let's see if you can solve the
> problem by using the four steps we just talked about."

Description of Desirable Behavior
The teacher describes or has an off-task pupil describe positive learning behavior that should replace ongoing deviant behavior.

> "What is the classroom rule about talking loudly during seatwork
> periods?"

Empathic Response
A teacher reaction which accurately reflects the meaning, and the
feeling behind, a pupil's comment or expression.

> "I guess it's pretty disappointing not to be able to go on the field
> trip when, as you say, you've looked forward to it for so long."

The preceding taxonomy of instructional skills provides a brief
description of many of the most basic interactive instructional skills.
When these skills are grouped in different combinations and sequences,
they can form a wide variety of instructional strategies.

INSTRUCTIONAL STRATEGIES

As defined in the previous section, instructional strategies are inten-
tional organizations (sequences) of interactive instructional skills for
the purpose of attaining the learning outcomes stated in the instructional objectives. In this section, a number of commonly employed
interactive strategies are listed and examined. In the list that follows,
a brief description of the generic instructional purposes to which each
strategy is applied is included opposite each strategy label. Although
the strategies listed represent only a small proportion of all of the
instructional strategies that teachers may employ (see Joyce and Weil,
1972), they should provide a reasonable sample of alternative methods
of instruction.

COMMONLY USED INSTRUCTIONAL STRATEGIES

Strategy	Generic Goals
1. Classic Lecture	To organize and disseminate basic facts, concepts, viewpoints, arguments, etc., to relatively large groups of learners.
2. Traditional Recitation (Question/Answer)	To engage pupils in active, teacher-controlled discussions of basic facts, concepts, theories, viewpoints, etc., to help learners form their own conceptualizations and arguments and to demonstrate knowledge or skill acquisition.
3. Multipurpose Small-Group Discussion	A more pupil-controlled, learner-centered counterpart of Strategy 2. Particularly useful for problem solving and decision making.
4. Role Plays	To engage students in active simulation exercises for the acquisition of social skills, clarification of values, or understanding of their own perceptions and attitudes and those of others.
5. Seatwork Practice	To provide opportunities for pupils to gain appropriate practice in a variety of basic academic tasks.
6. Inductive Teaching	To encourage the development of inductive cognitive processes, academic reasoning, theory construction, etc.
7. Science Inquiry	To stimulate student interest and skill in employing basic research and inquiry strategies.

Strategy	*Generic Goals*
8. Concept Attainment	To develop inductive reasoning from specific instances to larger concepts.
9. Nondirective Teaching	To emphasize development of self-instructional capacities. To aid in students' development of self-understanding, self-concept, and self-discovery.
10. Classroom Meeting	To develop personal responsibility and an awareness of classroom realities.
11. Behavior Modification	Systematic, empirically based methods of encouraging positive learning and social behaviors and of discouraging negative, disruptive actions.

All the instructional strategies in this list incorporate different sequences of discrete teaching skills. Some, such as traditional recitation use all three major skill categories (structuring, soliciting, reacting). Others, such as the classic lecture, and science inquiry, use only one major skill category (structuring skills for the lecture, reacting skills for the inquiry). Still other strategies, such as the multipurpose small-group discussion, while they use skills from all three categories, focus intensively on one or two key skills, such as promoting peer involvement and incorporating student response into the lesson. (A review of the taxonomy of instructional skills should help you determine why these skills are appropriate for these particular strategies.)

The remainder of this section is organized around a sequential description and analysis of each strategy in the preceding list. In each case, a general description of the instructional strategy, together with its theoretical basis and intended functions, is followed by a component skills table. The table lists most of the teaching skills that make up the strategy under discussion and gives examples of each skill as it is used in the specific strategy. While many of the strategies may use skills other than those listed in the component skills tables, the skills that are listed are considered to be fundamental to the successful classroom use of the strategy. Skills listed in the tables are organized by the three major skill areas of structuring, soliciting, and reacting.

Remember that instructional strategies are nothing more than purposeful arrangements of discrete instructional skills. If you gain a clear understanding of each skill and an appreciation of how and why the skills are grouped, you will be able to specify and practice any instructional strategy defined in this way. The strategy descriptions that follow aim to specify (1) the conceptualizations and understandings specific to each strategy (instructional cognitions), and (2) the exact interactive skills that comprise the strategy (instructional behaviors).

Classic Lecture

The classic lecture strategy is well known to almost all teachers. It consists of a relatively lengthy, largely one-way presentation of information by a teacher to a relatively large group of learners. If the classic lecture is organized and delivered well, it can be a very efficient means of communicating basic facts, concepts, viewpoints, and arguments of a particular area of knowledge to a wide audience. The effect of the classic lecture is different from that produced by having pupils read lecture materials and notes by themselves. The good lecturer affords students the opportunity of watching a competent thinker, researcher, and, most important, well-organized learner at work. The following component skills table highlights some of the most important interactive instructional skills that comprise an effective lecture. Notice that all classic lecturing skills are in the area of structuring.

COMPONENT SKILL	EXAMPLE
Structuring Skills Overview	"There are four main categories of mystery novels—romantic, classic whodunnit, detective, and intrigue. Today's lecture will examine each of these categories

Component Skill	Example
	in turn. Within each category, major characteristics of characters and plots will be examined.
Statement of Objectives	"By the end of today's talk, you should all be able to state the predominant character and plot types that define each of the four kinds of mystery novel."
Statement of Curriculum Links	"In discussing mystery novels, I will be making use of the general material about plots and characters that we focused on last week. I also may allude to some additional plot construction techniques, which we will examine in more detail in tomorrow's class."
Verbal Markers of Importance	"So, it is *absolutely essential* that you see the role of heroine through the eyes of the average middle-aged Victorian spinster."
Focusing by Rhetorical Question	"If this is all so much fun, why did anyone ever tire of reading gothic romantic mysteries?" (Pause) "Well, let's see what help we can get from Charles Dickins's description of the later Victorian mind."
Topic Summarization within a Lesson	"O.K., so in the romantic mystery we have a hero and heroine (both thoroughly enamoured of each other) who are typically unable to reach true love's fulfillment because of the atrocious conduct of one or more despic-

Component Skill	Example
	able characters, who refuse to be restrained by normal standards of right and wrong."
Statement of Transition	"Well, let's leave these romantic notions for now and turn to a related, but slightly more flexible, mystery form—the classic whodunnit."
Lesson Review	"Now that we've examined each mystery category, let's see what we have: the romantic form, complete with hero/heroine and clear-cut moral plots; the classic whodunnit, characterized by the all-powerful sleuth who is continually demonstrating the futility of legal/social misconduct. . . ."

Soliciting Skills
  (None in the classic lecture, although many lecturers will embed some small recitation strategies in their overall lecture format.)

Reacting Skills
  (None in the classic lecture strategy.)

Traditional Recitation

By far the most frequently used instructional strategy in school classrooms in North America is the recitation strategy. Recitation essentially means question-and-answer. There are many different forms of recitation, but all involve a teacher-controlled, two-way discussion of basic facts, concepts, theories, viewpoints, arguments, and values. While the traditional recitation is highly structured by the teacher, it does make provisions for pupils to generate and elaborate their own conceptualizations and arguments. It also provides opportunities for pupils to demonstrate knowledge and/or skill acquisition. Adaptable to classroom groups of many different sizes, the traditional recitation often is alternated with a more standard lecture strategy in any given instructional period. In such cases, the structuring skills used in recitation are essentially the same as those used in the lecture. It is the addition of soliciting and reacting skills that clearly demarcates the recitation from the lecture. A traditional recitation strategy should draw about equally from the three major skill areas.

COMPONENT SKILL	EXAMPLE
Structuring Skills (See skills listed under classic lecture. The same skills may be employed here, though probably less frequently.)	
Group Alerting Cues	"When I'm asking questions you should all be thinking hard, because I may ask any one of you to answer."
Soliciting Skills (Any of the specific soliciting skills listed in the Taxonomy of Instructional Skills may be used in any combination in a recitation lesson, depending on the specific objectives of the lesson: Random Recitation, Positive Questioning, and Pace can be particularly important.)	See examples from the Taxonomy of Instructional Skills.

COMPONENT SKILL	EXAMPLE
Reacting Skills (Again, any of the specific reacting skills listed in the Taxonomy of Instructional Skills may be used in any logical sequence that is appropriate to the instructional goals and activities. Incorporating Student Responses, Post-Response Wait Time, and Empathic Response can be particularly useful.)	See examples from the Taxonomy of Instructional Skills.

Multipurpose Small-Group Discussion

The small-group discussion is particularly useful for problem-solving, decision-making, and critical-thinking activities in which a high level of student participation and direction is required. In a well-run group discussion, the bulk of the conversation should come directly from students. Communicative exchanges should go from one pupil to another without the teacher acting as intermediary. In regular classroom settings, division of the class into several small groups often can permit a much greater degree of pupil involvement and overt practice in thinking and speaking. However, small-group discussions must be led skillfully if they are to achieve high levels of appropriate pupil involvement. The following component skills table lists a number of very important instructional skills for discussion-group leaders. These skills can enhance pupil involvement and increase the likelihood of pupil-to-pupil communication exchanges. While almost any instructional skill may be employed in a small-group discussion, I have listed only those that are most important in assisting a small group to enjoy its unique advantages.

COMPONENT SKILL	EXAMPLE
Structuring Skills	
Physical Arrangement	Arranging classroom furniture so that pupils who will work together are seated in a circular, conversational setting so that each pupil may clearly view and speak directly to every other pupil.
Group Alerting Cues	"Remember: When one person is talking pay very close attention so that you will be able to respond intelligently and in a way that extends the discussion."
(Other structuring skills, such as Statement of Objective, Topic Summation, and Lesson Review, also can, and should, be incorporated into a small-group discussion.)	
Soliciting Skills	
Opining or Valuing Questions	"What would any of you have done if you were faced with the situation that faced Oliver Twist at this point?"
Positive Questioning	Ask question; pause three to five seconds; call on specific pupil to respond.
Promoting Peer Involvement	"That point of Anna's reminds me of what you said earlier, Andy. Do you see any similarity there?" (Note: Promoting Peer Involvemen is a crucial skill in small-group discussions. It also may be done nonverbally by cuing other

COMPONENT SKILL	EXAMPLE
	pupils to respond through subtle facial expressions and hand gestures, all of which may convey "Well, what do you think about that?")
Reacting Skills Incorporating Student Responses into Lesson	"O.K., let's use Paul's idea and see whether it helps us solve this problem." *or* "I'll write down all the points you come up with so that you can discuss each of them later."
Post-Response Wait Time (This simple skill can be a powerful encouragement of pupil-to-pupil exchanges. If you always respond immediately as teacher, pupils will come to expect this and to sit passively as onlookers.)	Pausing at least three to five seconds after a pupil makes a statement in order to give other pupils an opportunity to respond or the same pupil an opportunity to continue.

Role Plays

Role plays engage pupils in active simulation exercises for the general purpose of acquiring specific skills, clarifying values, or understanding the perceptions, attitudes, and values of self and others. A tremendous variety of role-play simulation methods are available (see Boocock and Schild, 1968; Sarason and Sarason, 1973). Almost all role plays provide a quasi-realistic opportunity for pupils to practice and acquire new skilled performances or to become more familiar with viewpoints other than their own. The learning potential of role plays is summed up best by a part of Festinger's theory of cognitive dissonance (1957): "When actions conflict with cognitions, cognitions and perceptions tend to change to fit actions" (p. 6). In other words, a role play in which, for example, a member of a majority group experiences the situations that a member of a minority group may experience may have a greater impact on the value system of this student than a series of lectures on "The Nature of Prejudice."

COMPONENT SKILL	EXAMPLE
Structuring Skills Overview and Statement of Objectives (It is very important that role-play participants know exactly what the purposes and format of role plays are.) (Other structuring skills are used as required.)	"The purpose of "The Life Career Game" is to assist you in planning for the future—taking into account many factors, such as job opportunities, inflation, educational requirements, and so on. That's how the game is played. Remember: the game will run for ten rounds, and the team with the highest total score at the end is the winner."
Soliciting Skills (A wide variety of soliciting skills may be employed, but the skill of using Goal-Directed Prompts is particularly useful.) Goal-Directed Prompts	"Now, remember that each participant must make three separate attempts to solve the problem. How many have you made so far?"
Reacting Skills Informational Feedback	"I really like the way you initiated the conversation and the way you then listened very

COMPONENT SKILL	EXAMPLE
	attentively to Don's comments. You demonstrated two very important skills in making polite conversation."
Empathic Response	"When you were acting the part of the policeman, it seemed as if you were astonished at how logical that part suddenly seemed."
(Other reacting skills also may be useful depending upon the exact nature of the role play.)	

Seatwork Practice

Seatwork practice affords pupils the opportunity to gain appropriate practice and feedback on a wide variety of academic tasks. It is extremely important that directions for seatwork are clear. The teacher should use the strategy as an opportunity to observe carefully each pupil's direct performance on seatwork tasks. Teachers should move about the classroom during seatwork periods, reacting quietly to pupils' learning performances on an individual basis. The following instructional skills are useful for almost any seatwork.

COMPONENT SKILL	EXAMPLE
Structuring Skills (Stating Objectives and providing an Overview are as important here as in most strategies.)	

Component Skill	Example
Providing a Model for Student Self-Evaluation of Work	"Make sure that you double-check the correctness of each answer to the subtraction problems by adding the result to the subtracted number. You should always obtain the original number that you subtracted from."
Verbal Markers of Importance	"It is critical that you go through each of the problem solution steps in sequence."
Soliciting Skills (The following skills are used most often on a one-to-one basis during seatwork.)	
Prompting Question	"Take your time and see whether you can say the sound for each letter one at a time. The sound for *a* is? Ah . . ."
Showing Work	"O.K., show me exactly what you did."
Reacting Skills Informational Feedback with Justification	"When you take the time to put an obvious line to the left at the bottom of the letter *g*, it shows everyone that you mean *g*, not *q*."
Descriptive Praise	"You're being very careful to follow each step in turn, and as a result you're getting a lot of correct answers. You're getting to be a good worker. "
Description of Desirable Behavior	"It's really important to work hard during seatwork periods so that each of us learns a lot and helps others learn a lot by not disturbing them."

Inductive Teaching

Inductive teaching encourages the development of academic skills in reasoning and theory construction. Such strategies encourage pupils to work from the evidence they discover through their own senses, toward more abstract theoretical principles that apply to directly observable phenomena. A simple case of this inductive process occurs when pupils are required first to *identify* some basic information (data); then are encouraged to *explain* the data by relating one point to another (drawing cause-and-effect relationships); and, finally, are required to make *inferences* and form *hypotheses* that go beyond the information at hand. The work of Hilda Taba (1966) presents a much wider model of inductive teaching than the basic inductive teaching strategy just discussed. I recommend her book to anyone who wishes to examine inductive teaching methods in greater detail. As should be clear from the following component skills table, inductive instructional strategies are almost totally composed of soliciting skills. Inductive teaching consists largely of systematic movement from fact recall questions to conceptual questions and, finally, to opining and valuing questions. Reacting skills are also important insofar as they encourage pupil responses and incorporate these responses into the ongoing lesson.

Component Skill	Example
Structuring Skills	
(A very simple Overview usually suffices.)	"Today's discussion will concern the balance of power currently existing among the nations of the world."
Soliciting Skills	
Fact Recall Questions	"How many countries did we classify last time as Western, Communist, Third World, and Neutral?"
	"Which countries, if any, within each group might be considered major military powers?"

Component Skill	Example
Conceptual Questions	"How do the political ideologies of each group relate to their international policies?" "Why are the U.S.A. and U.S.S.R. involved so often in other countries' problems?"
Opining or Valuing Questions (In the case of Inductive Teaching, such questions ask pupils to speculate and theorize as well as state their own opinions.)	"What general principle concerning the role of superpowers in this regard would you be prepared to make?" "Can you imagine what would happen if Cuba joined the Western Bloc? What would our theory say about this?"
Redirection (A great deal of redirection of the previous questions would occur in any good Inductive Teaching strategy in order to involve many pupils.)	"All right, can someone else carry that idea a bit further?" "Tom, you don't agree. Tell us why." "What do you think, Bert?" "Brenda?" "Carl?"
Positive Questioning	Ask question; pause; call on reciter.
Reacting Skills Descriptive Praise	"That's one good reason why the U.S. might resist such a move."
Incorporating Student Responses into the Lesson	"You're saying that each superpower must be viewed as being equally strong as all other superpowers. Let's see whether we can work with your idea for a few minutes."

Science Inquiry

Science inquiry strategies have been developed largely as a result of Joseph Schwab's work in biology curriculum (1965). Science inquiry attempts to foster student awareness of the scientific process and the nature of scientific investigation. In most forms of inquiry teaching, students are presented with an area of investigation (e.g., a simple experiment, the description of a particular phenomenon) that contains a particular difficulty or problem (e.g., water doesn't fall from an inverted glass when the glass is covered with a tissue). Students then are stimulated to speculate about the problem and ways of clearing up the difficulty it presents. The teacher's role is to react to pupil statements and activities in ways that help pupils to generate hypotheses, interpret data, develop constructs, and engage generally in the process of scientific inquiry. In most cases, teacher reactions take the form of questions that elicit further pupil speculation and inquiry.

COMPONENT SKILL	EXAMPLE
Structuring Skills	
Inducing Set or Providing a Common Basis for Consideration (Other than this, very little formal structuring occurs.)	A specific problem or difficulty is posed by demonstration or verbal description.
Soliciting Skills	
Opining Questions (Usually in response to pupil statements or actions. The more open-ended the inquiry, the fewer prompts contained in the questions.)	"What did you decide about muscle size and muscle strength?" "From the data presented, what would you say is the strongest muscle in the human body?"
Judgmental Questions	"So, what do you base that conclusion on?" "Would the same thing happen if we'd used a mammal in the experiment instead of a reptile? Why?"

COMPONENT SKILL	EXAMPLE
Positive Questioning	Always avoid answering your own questions. Leave the questions for the pupils to work with.
Reacting Skills (Very little formal reacting other than indirectly through the questioning techniques discussed earlier.)	
Incorporating Student Responses into the Lesson	"You made a point just now about muscle size. How does your point apply to this problem?"

Concept Attainment

There are a great many different strategies for concept attainment (see Becker, Englemann, and Thomas, 1971; Bruner, Goodnow, and Austin, 1967; Taba, 1967) that have been employed to develop student skills in inductive reasoning. While many of these strategies are quite complex, almost all of them include the basic strategy to be discussed here. This strategy starts with the structured presentation of a wide variety of positive and negative exemplars of a particular concept. Students are then questioned about the nature of the concept and are encouraged to speculate by comparing and contrasting their hypotheses. In this way, for example, young children can be taught the concept of "mammal" by presenting them with a variety of objects (and perhaps pictures of objects), only some of which are mammals, and indicating in some way which ones are and which are not examples of the "mammal" concept. After this kind of exposure, learners are asked, as part of a *game,* to see whether they can say why some examples are mammals and others are not. The teacher encourages pupils to compare their hypotheses about the concept and to select examples of mammals and nonmammals from other presentations. When the defining characteristics of the concept have been voiced, the teacher can summarize the concept and conclude the lesson.

Component Skill	Example
Structuring Skills	
Verbal Markers of Importance	"So, some kind of hair or fur might be *very important.*"
Inducing Set	Presentation of positive and negative instances with an indication of whether each is or is not an instance of the concept to be learned.
(Other structuring skills may be incorporated as required.)	
Soliciting Skills	
Conceptual Questions	"What are the basic differences between these two animals?"
Judgmental Questions	"Why do you say that a whale isn't a mammal? Can you tell us how you made this decision?"
(Other skills such as Redirection, Probing, Peer Involvement, and Positive Questioning are as important here as they are in any questioning strategy is which enthusiastic pupil involvement is desired.)	
Reacting Skills	
(Almost any combination of Descriptive Praise, Informational Feedback, and Incorporating Student Response should work nicely.)	

Nondirective Teaching

The most frequently employed strategies of nondirective, or student-centered, teaching are derived from the theoretical work of Carl

Rogers (1969). More so than any of the strategies considered thus far, nondirective teaching makes almost exclusive use of reacting skills. The major purposes of nondirective teaching are (1) to encourage the development of pupil self-understanding, self-concept, and self-discovery, and (2) to assist pupils in developing self-instructional capabilities. In order to encourage self-exploration and the development of self-instructional skills, the nondirective teacher establishes an acceptant classroom climate within which students are free (within certain reasonable limits) to determine their own instructional objectives and to enact their innate learning strategies (potentials). The teacher can create such a climate by reacting to student learning and exploratory behaviors in ways that assume the students' frames of reference. The teacher should attempt to help students clarify their attitudes and feelings by reflecting these attitudes and feelings back to the learners as they are accepted and perceived by the teacher. In addition to this kind of empathic reflection, nondirective teachers act as open-ended, intellectual resource persons in the classroom. Rogers's major educational text, *Freedom to Learn* (1969), is essential reading for anyone truly interested in nondirective teaching strategies.

COMPONENT SKILL	EXAMPLE
Structuring Skills	
Physical Arrangement (Generally, little formal structuring is done through a teacher's direct classroom behavior. Rather, the teacher is responsible for arranging warm, interesting, and stimulating learning environments and materials.)	
Soliciting Skills	
(Little in the way of formal questions, since the ways in which nondirective teachers respond to pupil actions tend to provide opportunities for	

COMPONENT SKILL	EXAMPLE
pupils to extend and elaborate their own personal understanding.)	
Opining or Valuing Questions	"I wonder whether you can tell us how you feel about that poem?"
Reacting Skills	
Empathic Response	"You're really happy that you were able to solve that problem. It's a pretty good feeling to know that you can do things all by yourself." "So, it sounds like you're pretty concerned with Lord Jim's situation and perhaps wondering what you would do in his place."
Incorporating Student Responses into Lesson	"Jamie has suggested that we try a new strategy. Perhaps if we all listen to him, he can tell us more about it."

Classroom Meetings

One of the most powerful ways in which teachers can become involved with pupils in classrooms is through the classroom meeting. William Glasser (1969) has advocated three types of classroom meetings: (1) *social problem-solving meetings,* which attempt to solve individual and group problems; (2) *open-ended meetings,* which allow discussion of any area related to the lives of individual pupils; and (3) *educational-diagnostic meetings,* which are concerned with evaluating what pupils know about the classroom curriculum and the strategies pupils are using to learn and teachers are using to teach. Glasser claims that frequent use of classroom meetings helps to ensure responsible teacher-pupil interactions that lead to the kind of social involvement necessary for a well-managed classroom. All classroom meetings, whatever their specific purpose, require teachers to employ sound skills of physical arrangement, a variety of open-ended valuing or opining questions, skills that promote peer involvement, and reactions that are encouraging and nonjudgmental. For more specific information concerning classroom meetings, the reader is referred to Glasser's major text, *Schools Without Failure* (1969).

COMPONENT SKILL	EXAMPLE
Structuring Skills	
Physical Arrangement	Facilitate pupil-to-pupil communication by arranging the group in a circle so that everyone can see everyone else. Facilitate the meeting by using specific seating arrangements— (e.g., separate talkative pupils, sit beside a disruptive pupil to control through physical proximity, etc.).
Statement of Objectives	"In this group meeting you are free to talk about anything you want, or raise whatever issues you wish to raise. This is a time for us to get to know each other better and to learn ways in which we all can help each other learn and become active members of our classroom group."
Soliciting Skills	
Opining or Valuing Questions	"What do you think we can do about that problem? How can we help Jimmy to get more out of the class?'"

COMPONENT SKILL	EXAMPLE
Promoting Peer Involvement	"Thank you for an interesting suggestion. What do some others think about John's idea?"
Positive Questioning	Pausing after each question to give pupils ample opportunity to respond.
Reacting Skills	
Incorporating Student Responses into Lesson	"Mary and Anne have suggested. . . . Let's see whether we can work a bit more with their ideas."
Empathic Response	Do some paraphrasing of pupil responses and reflecting of affect. Don't overdo this, however, so that you prevent pupils from responding to each other.

Behavior Modification

While there are many behavior modification strategies employed in classrooms (see O'Leary and O'Leary, 1977), almost all of these strategies attempt to reinforce productive social and academic actions and generally ignore or curtail (through classroom rules and contracted consequences) off-task, disruptive actions. Formal use of behavior modification should be undertaken with full awareness of operant learning procedures and ethical safeguards (e.g., see Axelrod, 1977; Thoresen, 1973). However, the central idea of behavior modification—active encouragement and promotion of productive pupil behaviors—is useful to any effective teacher. The reacting skill of descriptive praise is an excellent way to reinforce or cue positive social and academic behaviors in the classroom.

Component Skill	Example
Structuring Skills	Everyone in the class should understand clearly the classroom conduct rules and academic criteria. This may be accomplished in a variety of ways (see O'Leary and O'Leary, 1977).
Reacting Skills Descriptive Praise	"Everyone is sitting quietly and working hard at the assignment. It's nice to see all of you doing such a good job at learning new things." "When you couldn't get the answer, you very calmly rechecked each step in your solution until you found the error. You've really learned how to help yourself do well."

There undoubtedly are many instructional strategies in addition to those which have been depicted in this section. The important point to remember is that all such strategies consist of purposeful sequences of discrete instructional skills and can be analyzed and conceptualized in terms of their constituent skills. In the final section of this chapter I will examine the importance of this kind of skill analysis for the acquisition of instructional strategies and behaviors.

INSTRUCTIONAL STYLES

Instructional style refers to the sum total of all of the characteristics, mannerisms, and unique personal qualities of an individual teacher. These characteristics are communicated to pupils in a variety of subtle ways. While instructional skills and strategies describe discrete teacher actions and the ways in which such actions may be grouped and sequenced, instructional styles describe basic personal qualities. Skills and strategies refer to what a teacher *does*; style refers to what a teacher *is*. In many ways, instructional styles are much less changeable than instructional skills and strategies. Consider the relative permanence of instructional style as you examine the following list of style dimensions. Many of the style labels in this list could be used to describe specific actions or short-term demeanors. For our purposes, however, they are intended to apply to relatively enduring personality characteristics that have some degree of consistency across situations and people. As the dimensions list indicates, teachers show great differences along style continua. These differences can be expected to color instructional skills and strategies significantly as they are used by individual teachers.

INSTRUCTIONAL STYLE DIMENSIONS

Analytic——General

Abrupt——Courteous

Encouraging——Critical

Doubting——Confident

Natural——Formal

Apathetic——Enthusiastic

Lively——Dull

Uncertain——Decisive

Controlled——Random

Gruff——Gentle

Cold——Warm

Fair——Biased

Self-Centered——Altruistic

Active——Passive

Capricious——Consistent

Easy-Going——Temperamental

Procrastinating——Punctual

Responsive——Aloof

Patient——Hurried

Spontaneous——Predictable

Close-Minded——Tolerant

Quick——Deliberate
Dishevelled——Orderly
Carefree——Troubled
Removed——Involved
Understanding——Insensitive
Retentive——Forgetful
Cooperative——Difficult
Humorous——Serious
Quiet——Boisterous
Talkative——Reticent
Straightforward——Roundabout
Plain——Vivacious
Complicated——Simple
Concrete——Abstract
Fanciful——Practical
Stubborn——Impatient
Shy——Outgoing
Thrifty——Wasteful
Energetic——Lax
Showy——Ordinary
Comfortable——Fidgety
Anxious——Relaxed
Rigid——Flexible

As you look carefully through this obviously incomplete list of style dimensions, you should be able to think of examples of the kinds of things that "stubborn," "patient," "warm," and "flexible" people do. However, it also should be apparent that such labels, as they are commonly employed, tend to go beyond an individual's actions to refer more pointedly to his or her basic character. While it is not true that styles cannot be modified, it is true that styles, as compared with skills and strategies, are relatively difficult to modify. When such modifications do occur, they are typically the result of second-order changes that are stimulated by basic alterations in skills and strategies. In short, if you wish to change your personal style, you are best advised to alter your skills and strategies. With constant effort, such changes gradually will show some effect on your overall style.

It is interesting to note that many people involved in teaching view instructional style as innate—"a born teacher," "either you've got it or you don't," "a natural." While such opinions undoubtedly are pleasant to those who are judged as having such an ability, there is nothing about instructional style that necessarily implies innateness. Many seemingly basic personal characteristics may be the result of extended processes of individual learning and development that have been active for twenty years or more before a person turns to teaching as a profession. Thus, it would be unreasonable to expect drastic changes in individual style in a relatively brief span of professional training or initial classroom experience. Twenty or thirty years of learning and development are not so easily or expediently altered, and such characteristics, whatever their origin, are likely to change very gradually.

Probably the best way in which to alter instructional style is first to become aware of your own style qualities and their likely effects on pupils. Should you decide that you would benefit from modification of one or more of these qualities, your best bet is to select a number of basic teaching skills or strategies that seem related to the characteristic(s) you wish to change and to implement a specific skill modification and acquisition program. For example, should you wish to become less "impatient" and more "encouraging," you might attempt to acquire skills such as "post-question wait time," "good pacing," "descriptive praise," and "incorporating student responses into the lesson." These skills are clearly related to increased patience and encouragement. By altering these skills systematically, you can expect, over time, to elicit changes in the style variables you are attempting to alter. The rule of thumb here is, "Change skills, and style changes gradually will follow."

Of course, awareness and knowledge of teaching style also may be used as a basis for making decisions about skill acquisition and use. Earlier in this chapter I spoke briefly about the importance of matching skills and strategies to style in order to ensure that all levels of teacher interaction (skills, strategies, style) are in harmony. This is a very important notion that teachers should understand clearly. Matching skills and strategies to style is meaningless if you attempt such matching before you acquire the necessary skill. Only after you have acquired and used specific skills or strategies can you determine whether they are supported well by your basic teaching style. To discard out of hand any instructional skill with which you have no personal experience represents decision making based on *ignorance*. The best policy is to work diligently at acquiring the skill or strategy and to use it enough to overcome any initial awkwardness or unnatural feelings. Only then can you make an *informed decision* about whether the skill or strategy works effectively in relation to your curriculum objectives, pupils, and style. In this way, professional growth can be an exciting experiment.

In the final analysis, whether you are attempting to alter your instructional style or to match skills and strategies with style, or both, it is most important that you approach teaching with an *experimental attitude*. No one can force you to teach in a particular way. What you do as a teacher, and how well you do it, depends on your own ability to experiment continually with a variety of instructional skills, strategies, and styles. Don't be afraid to try different things. The only way to determine whether something will work for you is to try it and see.

THE ACQUISITION OF INSTRUCTIONAL BEHAVIORS

The real purpose of studying, analyzing, and depicting interactive instructional behaviors is, of course, to provide a basis for skill practice and acquisition. Knowing about discrete instructional skills and strategies is useful to preservice and in-service teachers because such knowledge (specific instructional cognitions) can assist in the acquisition of interactive teaching methods (instructional behaviors). There are three essential criteria that must be met in the acquisition of instructional behaviors: (1) precise *specification* of the skill(s) to be acquired; (2) ample provision for repeated *practice* of the skill(s) in real-life contexts; and (3) precise, constructive *feedback* about the skill(s) practice (McDonald, 1969).

Specification of skills is important because it is impossible to practice and acquire something without knowing exactly what it is. Such knowledge, in the form of cognitions about specific forms of instructional behavior, is absolutely indispensable. Practice or experience alone (i.e., without specification) may or may not lead to effective skill acquisition. Further, inadequate specification of skills will prevent you from identifying and comprehending potentially useful feedback about those skills. The descriptions of structuring, soliciting, and reacting skills that appeared earlier in this chapter constitute a first step toward defining and depicting a variety of instructional behaviors. In addition to such written descriptions, direct observation of teachers using these skills in simulated and actual classroom contexts is invaluable for acquiring information about the exact parameters of discrete instructional behaviors, and provides a useful model for your own skill practice. I encourage readers to study carefully the instructional skills and strategies outlined in this chapter, to discuss them with others, and to arrange for opportunities to observe the teaching behaviors of other classroom teachers in relation to these skills and strategies. These undertakings will strengthen instructional cognitions about specific instructional behaviors and their contributions to basic instructional processes.

Once you are well informed about the specific actions that make up instructional behaviors, it is essential that you *practice* these actions repeatedly. Such practice might begin with a few awkward attempts to produce appropriate verbal and nonverbal behaviors alone—in front of a mirror, to fellow teachers or student teachers, or in small *microteaching* simulations. Try to make each practice element as realistic as possible. As you become more proficient and comfortable with a particular skill, you may want to construct small lessons that incorporate these skills. These lessons can be taught to fellow teachers or student teachers and may be audiotaped or videotaped. Gradually, as the use of the skill becomes more natural (i.e., consistent with your own basic teaching style), you undoubtedly will want to extend your skill practice to real-life classroom contexts. This is theoretically what practice teaching (e.g., field placements in training programs, on-site in-service practice) is all about.

Of course, practice is only as good or useful as the *feedback* you receive as a result. We already have discussed feedback as an essential ingredient in curriculum presentation to pupils. The same principles apply to feedback for the purpose of acquiring instructional behaviors. Whether feedback comes from mirrors, fellow preservice or in-service teachers, teacher trainers or supervisors, audiotape or videotape, self-observation, or some combination of these methods, it should be specific, immediate, constructive, and encouraging or positive in nature. Your task as a skill learner is to make yourself open and receptive to feedback and to modify and organize your future experimentation with skills according to such feedback. This is the process by which you can acquire new instructional skills and strategies, or (in the long term) modify your own instructional style.

Much more will be said about skill practice and acquisition in Chapter 5, which contains a very specific model of specifying, practicing, and obtaining feedback about instructional skills (see Chapter 5, section on *Formative Evaluation Model*). In the meantime, one overall truth about skill acquisition should be restated. *The process of skill acquisition is a process of experimentation.* For most teachers, it is impossible to know whether or not a particular teaching skill will be useful until they first acquire it and then learn to use it with some degree of expertise. It is often tempting to limit skill practice to a few skills that initially seem to be consistent with our view of ourselves and our capabilities, or with our philosophical or affective beliefs about what instruction is and should be. While there is absolutely nothing wrong with such views (we all have them), we should not allow them to deter us from extensive, committed practice of a wide variety of instructional behaviors. Once we have acquired a broad repertoire of such behaviors, we can always select those with which we are most competent, comfortable, or philosophically attuned.

As was mentioned previously, the ultimate goal of skill acquisition is to match instructional skills to personal teaching styles and beliefs in appropriate and powerful ways. The important thing to realize is that, if you want to maximize this matching, you should keep an open, experimental attitude until you have developed a broad base of skills from which to work. Once again, to make decisions about what skills you will and won't use before you give yourself the opportunity to acquire a full instructional repertoire is tantamount to making decisions based on ignorance. Therefore, it is extremely important that you engage in enlightened, open-minded inquiry that will help you discover your own strengths and weaknesses.

If you undertake the acquisition of instructional behaviors in this manner, the potential for reducing instructional stress (see Chapter 2) is tremendous. With a clear comprehension of a variety of instructional skills, strategies, and styles (specific instructional cognitions), there is little reason to experience stress as a consequence of not knowing what to do. With the acceptance of an open, experimental attitude predicated on the belief that it is possible to become an increasingly competent instructor (general instructional cognitions), the stress-inducing effects of defeatist self-talk and beliefs (see Chapter 2) are minimized. Finally, with the actual execution of effective instructional behaviors during interactive instruction, stress associated with behavioral incompetence and uncertainty is effectively removed.

QUESTIONS AND RESPONSES

1. *Q:* Isn't this skill approach awfully mechanistic? Surely teaching is as much an art as a science. Won't too much analysis spoil the essential wholeness that makes good teaching what it is?

R: The reason for breaking down entire teaching sequences into discrete recognizable elements (skills) is to assist teachers and prospective teachers in learning extensive instructional repertoires. Learning is facilitated when what is to be learned is specified clearly so as to permit realistic practice and feedback. Obviously, the point of skill analysis is not to perform mechanical skills out of context, but rather to integrate each newly acquired skill gradually into an effective overall instructional style. However, effective personal styles do not come about all at once or by some magical process. For many prospective teachers, learning a few basic skills is often the first step toward discovering their stylistic potential. Knowing how to do a few basic things well can help create a sense of personal confidence that is invaluable to the development of powerful instructional styles.

As for the question of art versus science, teaching is probably a little bit of both. The emphasis on matching discrete, learnable skills to more natural styles in this chapter is a recognition of teaching as partially science and partially art. You never should be afraid to analyze what you do, as long as the overall purpose of such analyses is to build stronger and more powerful syntheses.

2. *Q:* I don't really see why we need all this jargon to talk about a basic human activity such as teaching. Surely one can teach without knowing and using labels like "strategies," "soliciting," "reacting," "self-analysis," and so on.

R: Any discipline or area of human activity carries with it a specific vocabulary. Although too much jargon generally is not a good idea, there is a difference between too much jargon and enough jargon to permit meaningful exchanges among people in a discipline. It would be extremely inconvenient and time consuming, for instance, if you had to give a formal definition and several examples each time you wished to convey the concepts of descriptive praise or group alerting cues to a colleague. The advantage of taking some time initially to learn standard, nonexcessive jargon is that it permits easy and efficient exchanges between you and others in your discipline. When you share useful jargon, you share meaning. Knowing precisely what others in your discipline are talking about and being able to talk precisely to others about your own teaching experiences are invaluable aids to professional development. Don't be afraid of learning a bit of new language when doing so can be functional. Of course, by the same token, don't readily embrace meaningless, vague jargon just for the sake of "appearing professional." The rule of thumb should be that, if use of jargon is backed up by a specific, meaningful concept, the jargon is useful; otherwise, it is not.

Of course, it is possible to teach well without knowing any of this jargon. However, should you wish to work continually toward improving your teaching, no matter how good it is at present, being able to avail yourself of knowledge and ideas generated by others in the field usually demands some ability to communicate through specific jargon.

3. *Q:* I'm still not sure how curriculum presentation differs from interactive instructional skills and strategies.

R: *Curriculum* is a general term that refers to the arrangement and presentation of a course of study. As such it encompasses instructional goals, instructional materials and activities, teaching methods, and the interrelationships of these elements. Interactive instructional skills and strategies are part of curriculum—the part that refers specifically to what teachers actually do during classroom interactions.

4. *Q:* How do the preactive skills discussed in Chapter 3 link up with the interactive skills discussed in this chapter?

R: This is an extremely important question. Preactive skills determine what to teach, whereas interactive skills actually teach it. (See Chapter 3 for a discussion of why student-centered views of instruction are often more useful than teacher-centered views.) The important point to remember is that there always should be a tight interface between preactive and interactive skills. Interactive skills always should be determined from a careful analysis of preactive instructional objectives. The choice of interactive skills is dependent on which teaching methods are best suited to helping pupils to learn the skills and knowledge contained in specific instructional objectives. Thus, it would be reasonable to select one set of interactive skills to help pupils understand the feelings of minority group members, and another set to help them distinguish triangles from rectangles. Matching interactive skills to the products of preactive skills (i.e., instructional objectives) helps to ensure that instructional purposes will be matched appropriately with instructional methods.

5. *Q:* When I look at all the strategies presented in this chapter, it seems to me that some are better than others almost without qualification. Some of them just seem to provide more healthy, honest ways of interacting with kids in classrooms. Is this so?

R: I know of no strategy that is consistently superior to all others, whether for humane, ethical, or practical reasons, across a wide array of instructional objectives and individual learners. For teaching to be both effective and good, it must facilitate the pupil learning performances contained in instructional objectives. Further, it must do this in ways that do not harm the learner or dampen the learner's enthusiasm for further learning. Instructional objectives may vary greatly across psychomotor, cognitive, and affective domains, and pupil entry capabilities may represent these variances. Both of these facts make it impossible to say that some strategies are consistently better than others for all objectives and learners. Healthy instruction is good, effective instruction. Nothing is more honest than this. As we will see in the next chapter, instructional effectiveness is not dependent on the selection of one strategy over others. Rather, it is largely a matter of selecting the single strategy that is *best suited* to your own teaching strengths, the current capabilities of your pupils, and the nature of the instructional objectives.

6. *Q:* Can't you get into trouble if you plan just one strategy for a given lesson?

R: I guess it's always possible to get into trouble in any discipline, and teaching is certainly no exception. As we have seen in Chapter 2, the ability to cope with adversity is one of the strongest cards in a good teacher's deck. One very effective way to cope is to plan for eventualities other than "everything going absolutely perfectly." With respect to instructional strategies, it is probably an excellent idea to construct a main strategy that is based on your knowledge of relevant pupil and curriculum information. An alternative strategy (which may be a variation of the main strategy) also can be planned just in case everything doesn't work in exactly the manner intended. I've seen numerous teachers use alternative planning very effectively. For example, I recently attended an instructional workshop during which the teacher began one session by asking an open-ended, opining question. When responses were very slow in coming (even with good post-question wait time), the teacher suggested that we divide ourselves into small groups to discuss the question. Later, when we came back into the large group, the same question produced a frenzy of responses. I thought this was a very good example of planning a main strategy and supplementing it with a powerful back-up strategy. I strongly urge you to consider adopting such a practice when you plan your own strategies for specific lessons.

7. *Q:* I can see how it is possible to control the class to meet your objectives if you use some of the more directive strategies, such as lecture or recitation. But I don't see how you can similarly guarantee your objectives if you use nondirective teaching strategies.

R: It sounds a bit like you're forgetting that instructional objectives are not just for your convenience as a teacher. The entire notion of performance-referenced objectives is to keep instruction centered around the learner. Instructional strategies simply are purposeful organizations of teacher actions that are intended to facilitate the learning performances contained in student-centered objectives. If the goal of instruction were simply to cover material, then more directive strategies such as the lecture might indeed be better equipped to meet such an objective. The goals of instruction, however, are not "coverage" goals. Rather, they are goals that evolve around pupil acquisition of knowledge and skills and resultant changes in their learning performances. Coverage does not in any way guarantee effective acquisition or learning. For many worthwhile objectives, nondirective strategies provide opportunities for essential pupil activity and feedback that might be absent if directive strategies were employed.

It is more difficult at first to control exactly what happens when you are a less directive teacher, but this is mostly because many teachers are not as familiar with nondirective methods as they are with directive strategies. With practice and careful analysis, nondirective instructional strategies can be used just as purposefully as directive ones to help students meet objectives. Obviously, some objectives (such as "Pupils will discuss their main ideas with each other, will listen carefully to the ideas of others, and will be able accurately to summarize each other's opinions") are less approachable through standard directive strategies, such as lecture and recitation, than are other objectives (such as "Each pupil will be able to state at least three causes of the First World War").

8. *Q:* I can't believe that what a teacher *is* (style) isn't more important than what a teacher *does* (skills and strategies).

R: Teaching *style* is very important, but teaching *skills and strategies* are equally important. If you stop for a moment and think about people you like and dislike, people you respect and don't respect, and so on, you probably will realize that you feel about them the way you do largely because of what they do and say when you are with them. Since none of us truly can look inside another person, these behaviors and the way they affect us are all we really have to go by.

When we talk about a person's style we usually are referring, at least in part, to what they actually do. As we have seen in this chapter, skills and strategies can affect style in a number of ways. When we talk about what a person *is*, we usually are referring to what he or she does and says in a wide variety of settings. What a person is also includes the subtle individual mannerisms that accompany the consistent aspects of personal behavior. A classroom teacher may be a very caring, warm person most of the time, but he or she still must be able to use skills and strategies in the classroom that are consistent with this basic style and that communicate this style to pupils. It is this consistent *matching* of skills and strategies to styles that is, perhaps, more important in teaching than any single skill, strategy, or style by itself.

SUGGESTED ACTIVITIES

1. After studying carefully the taxonomy of interactive instructional skills contained in this chapter, arrange to observe a number of teachers in actual classroom situations and see whether you can identify their use of any of the skills described. If you do not have easy access to public school classrooms, observe postsecondary, recreational, or continuing/adult education courses in your area. Make a special point of observing instructional skills used by

teachers in courses that you might be enrolled in yourself. Don't concern yourself with judging whether the teaching you observe is good or bad (much more will be said about this in the next chapter); just see whether you can describe the teaching in relation to the skills taxonomy.

2. Select three or four frequently used skills and, together with a friend, observe a teaching session. Note (on a separate piece of paper) each time the teacher uses one of these skills. Do this independently and, at the end of the class, compare notes with your friend. Did you see the same things? Why? Why not?

3. Practice teaching short lessons to a group of your peers. Tell an observer which instructional skills you are going to use, and allow the observer to take notes about your actual use of these skills during the lesson. Discuss the observer's observations after each lesson.

4. Plan a few short lessons in which you attempt to make appropriate use of the learning principles of meaningfulness, activity, feedback, and organization.

5. Construct a complex, high-level cognitive objective appropriate for the grade level you are teaching or that you might wish to teach. Check to make sure that the objective is stated clearly in terms of what pupils will be able to do at the end of the lesson that they can't do at the beginning of the lesson. Once you have done this, construct three different instructional strategies that might facilitate the learning performances in the objective. Describe the exact skill composition of each strategy. Which strategy would you use as a main strategy? Why?

6. Try to enact the main strategy developed in activity five in a regular classroom or in a microteaching setting with a group of peers. Have someone observe and record your use of the strategy in terms of its component skills. Are you really using the skills you intended to use? If so, do these skills come together to produce the learning effects you intended?

7. Arrange to observe the teaching performance of a friend or colleague. Record the interactive instructional skills being used. On the basis of the skills and the sequence in which they are used, how would you describe the overall instructional strategy employed? Perhaps more than one strategy was used. If so, how many strategies were used, and what were they?

8. How would you describe your own teaching style? Write as many descriptive adjectives as you can that seem to be applicable to your own teaching style. Ask one or two colleagues or friends to observe you in the act of teaching and to make a similar list of adjectives that describe their perceptions of your teaching style. Compare your list of style elements with their lists to check the reliability of your perceptions.

REFERENCES

Axelrod, S. 1977. *Behavior Modification for the Classroom Teacher.* New York: McGraw-Hill.

Becker, W.C.; Englemann, S.; and Thomas, D.R. 1971. *Teaching: A Course in Applied Psychology.* Chicago: Science Research Associates.

Bellack, A.A.; Kliebard, H.M.; Hyman, R.T.; and Smith, F.L. 1966. *The Language of the Classroom.* New York: Teachers College Press.

Boocock, S., and Schild, E.O. (eds.). 1968. *Simulation Games in Learning.* Beverly Hills, Calif: Sage Publications.

Borg, W.R. 1973. *Protocol Materials.* Utah Protocol Materials Project, Utah State University.

Bruner, J.; Goodnow, J.J.; and Austin, G.A. 1967. *A Study of Thinking.* New York: Science Editions.

Dinkmeyer, D., and Dreikurs, R. 1963. *Encouraging Children to Learn.* Englewood Cliffs, N.J.: Prentice-Hall.

Glasser, W. 1969. *Schools Without Failure.* New York: Harper and Row.

Festinger, L. 1957. *A Theory of Cognitive Dissonance.* Stanford, Calif.: Stanford University Press.

Joyce, B., and Weil, M. 1972. *Models of Teaching.* Englewood Cliffs, N.J.: Prentice-Hall.

Kounin, J.S. 1977. *Discipline and Group Management in the Classroom.* New York: Holt, Rinehart and Winston.

McDonald, F.J. 1969. *A Theoretical Model for the Use of Observational Learning in Acquiring Teaching Skill.* Paper presented at the American Educational Research Association Annual Meetings, Los Angeles.

Martin, J., and Walsh, J. 1979. "Self-Reinforcement and Self-Directed Learning." In *Self-Education,* edited by M. Gibbons, G. Phillips, and G. Ivany. Burnaby, B.C.: Simon Fraser University.

O'Leary, K.D., and O'Leary, S.G. 1977. *Classroom Management: The Successful Use of Behavior Modification.* New York: Pergamon Press.

Rogers, C. 1969. *Freedom to Learn.* Columbus, Ohio: Charles E. Merrill.

Sarason, I.G., and Sarason, B.R. 1973. *Modeling and Role-Playing in the Schools: A Manual with Reference to the Disadvantaged Student.* Los Angeles, Calif.: Human Interaction Research Institute.

Schwab, J. 1965. *Biology Teacher's Handbook.* Biological Sciences Curriculum Study. New York: John Wiley and Sons.

Taba, H. 1966. *Teaching Strategies and Cognitive Functioning in Elementary School Children.* San Francisco: San Francisco State College.

————. 1967. *Teacher's Handbook for Elementary Social Studies.* Reading, Mass.: Addison-Wesley.

Thoresen, C.E. (ed.). 1973. *Behavior Modification in Education.* N.S.S.E. Yearbook (Part I). Chicago: National Society for the Study of Education.

Underwood, B.J., and Swartz, R.W. 1960. *Meaningfulness and Verbal Learning.* Philadelphia: J.B. Lippincott.

Winne, P.H., and Martin, J. 1979. *Teaching Skills Handout.* Burnaby, B.C.: Simon Fraser University.

5

Evaluation of Instruction

The instructional behaviors and accompanying cognitions discussed in this chapter are used to determine whether the learning performances stated in instructional objectives (see Chapter 3) are attained by the curriculum presentations and interactive instructional skills and strategies discussed in the previous chapter. As we shall see, making determinations of this kind involves the systematic evaluation of both pupil learning and instructional effectiveness. This chapter begins with an examination of pupil learning assessments, moves on to consider evaluations of instructional effectiveness, and concludes with a discussion of how reasonable evaluation systems can be implemented in school classrooms (see Fig. 5.1). The evaluation systems presented are predicated on the notion that evaluation of instruction and learning must be viewed as a crucial element in the learning process per se. Evaluation should not be viewed as something to do only after active instruction and learning have occurred. Rather, it is important to keep in mind that evaluation is an ongoing process that should be integrated harmoniously with both preactive and interactive instructional elements. Careful evaluation of instruction and learning is essential if

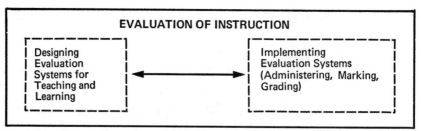

FIGURE 5.1   *The Evaluation Phase of Instruction*

teachers are to work continually toward improving the educational climate in their classrooms. Knowledge about the efficacy of teaching and learning actions is indispensable to progressive change in instructional systems.

EVALUATION OF PUPIL LEARNING

Probably the most misunderstood aspect of instruction is that which concerns the assessment of pupil learning. Otherwise competent teachers are often confused and bewildered by the expectation that they must evaluate the learning progress of their pupils. Evaluation is often seen as inhumane, counterproductive, or simply wasteful of valuable teaching and learning time. Unfortunately, such views, while they may be very well intentioned, tend to be centered around certain common misunderstandings of the basic principles that underlie evaluation methods. Without a clear understanding of these principles it is impossible to recognize good and bad applications of them. Consequently, certain evaluation procedures that are essentially bad implementations of evaluation principles readily become confused with any attempt to evaluate pupil learning. It is possible to evaluate pupil learning in ineffective and harmful ways. It also is possible to create and implement evaluation systems that are beneficial parts of classroom instructional programs for both learners and teachers. Since confusion about evaluation can be a major contributor to the professional stress that many teachers experience, this section will be devoted to an elucidation of the basic principles underlying sound evaluation systems. What is presented is not a detailed treatment of test and measurement theory or test construction. While such information is extremely important, it is dealt with exceptionally well in a variety of readily available works devoted entirely to these topics (e.g., Grunland, 1976; Thorndike and Hagen, 1977).

Purposes of Evaluating Pupil Learning

Three main purposes of pupil learning evaluation are often cited: (1) classification, (2) diagnosis, and (3) feedback. *Classification* refers to the use of tests to determine which pupils are high achievers ("A" students), average achievers ("B" and "C" students), and low achievers ("D" and "F" students) in particular curriculum areas or in all curriculum areas. Such classifications are often used to determine pupils' progress through various levels or grades, to determine admissions to universities and other postsecondary institutions, or to determine eligibility for academic awards and scholarships.

Diagnosis refers to the use of tests (more precisely, the information furnished by tests) to determine specific areas of learning or teaching weakness. Once determined, such weaknesses may be remedied before they worsen. Tests are used to determine exactly what pupils know and do not know, can and cannot do. Once such information is available, specialized instruction may be arranged to fill in large gaps in pupils' knowledge or abilities. In a sense, diagnosis is a kind of classification, but it is classification with the expressed purpose of eliminating the very basis on which it rests. Rather than classifying groups of pupils so that they can be segmented further in terms of abilities, diagnosis attempts to identify pupils with learning deficits so that such deficits can be dealt with effectively.

Feedback refers to the use of tests to provide pupils and teachers with information and motivation that will assist them in improving their learning or teaching performances. (Feedback already has been discussed in some detail in the previous chapter.) It now should be obvious that immediate, accurate, correctional, and encouraging feedback about unsuccessful learning performances can provide students with the information they need to become successful. Feedback based on test results also is useful to the teacher for gauging personal efficacy as a facilitator of learning (more will be said about this function of evaluation later in the chapter).

While evaluations of pupil learning can be employed quite legitimately for purposes of classification, diagnosis, and feedback, it is important to understand the emphasis of each function. Evaluation for classification is not concerned directly with facilitating the improvement of individual pupil learning. Rather, it tends to be *summative* in nature. On the other hand, evaluation for diagnosis and feedback is concerned directly with fostering improvements in both learning and teaching. In this sense, evaluative functions of diagnosis and feedback are integrated closely with ongoing learning and instructional programs and thus tend to be *formative* in nature. If teachers are concerned with optimizing the learning potentials of pupils on a day-to-day basis, they would do well to focus their evaluation efforts on diagnosis and feedback functions rather than classification.

Processes of Evaluating Pupil Learning

Whether evaluation systems perform classification or diagnostic and feedback functions is determined largely by the nature of the basic evaluation processes of *sampling* and *comparison*. Any type of evaluation demands that something is sampled and then compared with something else. In evaluations of classroom learning, what is sampled is the learning performances of individual pupils in relation to a representative selection of instructional objectives and content. In other words, any evaluation of pupil learning must sample the pupil learning performances stated in instructional objectives and addressed in interactive classroom activities. Evaluation is pointless if it is not tied to preactive objectives and interactive curriculum presentation. If such ties or connections are not made, there will be no way of determining accurately either what should be evaluated or whether what is being evaluated is consistent with what has been taught. All three elements—objectives, interactive instruction, and evaluation—must be in harmony. If a teacher gives a multiple-choice test of factual information concerning Bach's life to pupils who have been engaged in a general music appreciation curriculum whose objective is recognition of melodies and techniques shared by past and contemporary composers, it is guaranteed that most pupils will fail. This is because the test items do not sample a selection of pupil learnings relevant to the course of study undertaken. Any test of pupil learning must sample pupil learning performances in relation to what has been taught. A good way of doing this is to determine first how much instructional time has been devoted to major instructional objectives. With this information, a teacher can create an evaluation device that samples relevant pupil learning in proportion to the instructional time devoted to it. This procedure prevents teachers from employing a final examination based entirely on quadratic equations, when the algebra course being evaluated devoted only a third of its time to quadratic equations. (More will be said about sampling pupil learning performances in the next section.)

Once the pupil learning performances have been sampled, the samples (more precisely, the evaluation results yielded by such sampling) must be compared with something else so as to furnish a determination of how well or poorly each pupil has learned. An individual learner's performance can be measured against three major standards: (1) the performance of *other pupils* (norms), (2) the performance *criteria* stated in instructional objectives, or (3) the *same pupil's* learning *performances* before instruction. Obviously, many different combinations of these standards also can be employed.

When samples of a pupil's learning performances are compared with samples of the learning performances of other pupils, the evaluation system is said to be *norm-referenced*. When criteria from instructional objectives are employed as comparison standards, the evaluation system is said to be *criterion-referenced*. The third method, of comparing a pupil's current to past learning performances, is referred to as *self-referenced* evaluation. Not surprisingly, the process of sampling and comparison selected by a teacher is often the most critical determinant of the overall purpose of the evaluation system. This is true irrespective of the actual intent of the teacher and may explain why many teachers who do not fully understand the underlying principles and processes of evaluation find evaluation so frustrating and confusing. Stated simply, norm-referenced testing generally leads to classification, whereas criterion-referenced and self-referenced testing generally lead to feedback and diagnosis.

Reliability and Validity

Regardless of the purpose or process of a particular evaluation system, the system should be constructed so as to validate one essential aphorism: "If pupils truly know their 'stuff,' they will do well; if not, they will do poorly." This may sound harsh, but the short-term and long-term consequences of using tests on which pupils who do not know their stuff do well, while those who do know their stuff do poorly, can be very harmful to all parties concerned. Tests themselves do not harm or help pupils; rather, it is the way tests are used that either helps or hinders pupil learning and development. In order for constructive uses of evaluation information to have the most potential for enhancing learning, such information must be both *reliable* and *valid*. (While there are many kinds of reliability and validity—see, for example, Grunland, 1976; Thorndike and Hagen, 1977—only the basic issues as they affect classroom teachers are presented here.)

Reliability To be reliable, a test must yield consistent results. In other words, a reliable evaluation system will not evaluate Jimmy's learning performances positively at point A and negatively at point B when relevant instruction has not occurred between A and B. The reliability of tests may be affected by pupils' physical condition; pupils' preferences for oral, written, or activity tests; pupils' anxieties; and assorted transitory problems. The best way for a teacher to increase the likelihood that evaluation systems will be reliable is to evaluate frequently across different response modalities. Instead of relying on one final written examination to produce a reliable estimate of a pupil's learning in a semester-long course, a teacher should administer a variety of tests or evaluation instruments (some written, some oral, some observational) at frequent intervals throughout the course. A pupil's average performance on a variety of tests will generally yield a consistent (reliable) indication of the pupil's true learning. By sampling a pupil's learning performances at regular intervals, the occasional poor performance can be offset by other, more realistic estimates of that pupil's learning. Thus, frequent testing across a variety of pupil response modalities is much more likely to produce a reliable estimate of pupil learning than is less frequent, unimodal testing.

Validity To be valid a test must succeed in testing what it is intended to test. If a teacher tests a pupil's ability to use a computer by having the pupil label the parts of a computer on a printed diagram, we might expect such a test to be invalid in relation to its stated purpose. Labeling computer parts may be a valid indicator of a pupil's knowledge of computer parts, but it cannot be assumed that such knowledge is equivalent to the functional ability to use the computer. Whenever there is any degree of incongruence among instructional objectives (purposes), instructional activities, and pupil evaluation systems, the chances of obtaining invalid pupil evaluations are increased. Of course, a teacher can almost guarantee invalid evaluation of pupil learning by failing to state instructional objectives clearly. Unless there is a clear understanding on the part of both teacher and pupils about what learning is intended (and thus what examinations will test for), valid pupil evaluations are extremely unlikely.

To increase the likelihood that an evaluation device will measure what it is intended to measure, a teacher should do a *task analysis* (see Chapter 3) of the various performances required to complete the evaluation correctly. This enables the teacher to compare the learning performances required by the evaluation system with those addressed by the course of instruction. A good match is a reasonable indication of a valid evaluation system.

An evaluation system must be reliable before it has any chance of being valid. Thus, evaluation systems that involve frequent testing across different pupil response modalities, such that the testing is congruent with the instructional objectives and activities undertaken up to the time of each test, are likely to be both fair and accurate. Of course, all of this is an elaborate way of saying that evaluation should be viewed as an integral part of pupil learning rather than as something that occurs when learning is over. If evaluation is to have powerful diagnostic and feedback functions that will help to nurture learning in a formative, ongoing manner, such integration is indispensable.

Types of Tests

Generally speaking, there are three broad categories of tests: *standardized, formal,* and *informal.*

Standardized Tests   The standardization of a test involves the development of uniform procedures for administering and scoring the test. Standardized tests employ systematic methods of test construction and interpretation. Part of the construction of such a test involves administering it to a large and representative sample of the type of student for whom the test is designed. An individual's score has meaning only when compared with the scores of others. A *norm* is the score that indicates average or normal performance.

The special character of standardized tests makes them particularly useful in the evaluation of new instructional programs or procedures, in the assessment of long-term learning, and in the general assessment of student achievement and ability. The *Mental Measurements Yearbook* (Buros, 1972) provides critical reviews of standardized tests that are currently available.

Formal Tests   Formal tests include the usual types of teacher-made classroom tests. These tests are adapted more carefully to an individual teacher's instructional objectives and subject matter than are standardized tests. The performance of a student is compared only with either the performances of other students in the same class or the criteria contained in class-specific objectives. Formal tests are usually in the form of the *essay,* the *restricted response,* or the *structured response.* Each type can deal with a variety of objectives. Essay tests measure a student's ability to organize, synthesize, and apply information. Restricted response tests (completion, short-answer) deal with highly specific bits of information that enable a teacher to pinpoint exactly what a student knows. Structured response tests (multiple choice, true-false, matching) break down complex ideas into component parts and test students on various aspects of these ideas. Generally speaking, each variety of formal test is appropriate for testing a particular kind of learning; however, this is not always true. Some interesting exceptions to this generalization have been developed (e.g., true-false tests with the added feature of providing written rationales for specific responses). In addition, all types of learning, whether factual knowledge, analysis of ideas, or formulation of value judgments, are equally important at various stages of the educational process.

Informal Tests   Informal tests can be used for classroom evaluation without the usual paraphernalia of pens and papers. These tests are based on systematic (valid and reliable) observations of the verbal or nonverbal behaviors of students. Oral examinations at the graduate level in universities have long made use of this technique. Various behavioral categories and criteria are carefully defined, and scores are assigned in reference to these categories and criteria. With proper specification and systematic observation, questions of both quantity and quality of pupil interaction and participation can be adjudicated. The results of informal tests can be just as valuable as the results of formal tests. Unfortunately, the former may be more prone to abuse in that teachers may tend to forget to specify observational criteria and to relate these criteria uniformly to the performances of students.

Test Construction

Since most teacher-made classroom tests are of the formal variety, this section will include illustrations derived largely from this category. Three general cautionary points are fundamental to formal test construction:

1. In writing formal classroom tests, remember that student scores should reflect how well students accomplish the task, not how well they decipher your questions. Questions should be clear and unambiguous. "Trick" items that are intentionally confusing or that deal with obscure bits of information should be avoided.
2. It is often a good idea to give tests a trial run with the assistance of colleagues or other students. Such trials can remove "bugs" that could cost both you and your students a good deal of agony and frustration.
3. Remember to check tests against instructional objectives and activities. This avoids the common trap of spending most of the class time emphasizing certain things and then testing for others.

Restricted Response Tests The following is a brief series of tips on constructing restricted response test items (completion questions, short-answer questions).

A. *Completion Questions (Fill in the Blanks)*
- Only significant words should be omitted.
  Example: The law of (*inertia*) states that a body at rest tends to remain at rest, and a body in motion tends to remain in motion.
- Avoid "pat" answers that are cued by key words that precede the blank.
  Example: Thorndike viewed *learning* as a process of trial and error (*learning*).
- Avoid grammatical cues that delimit possible responses.
  Example: An engine that uses explosive gas as its energy source is called an (*internal combustion*) engine.
- Avoid mutilated statements that provide insufficient context.
  Example: (*Prejudice*) is the result of (*ignorance*), (*fear*), and (*self-centeredness*).
- In many cases, completion items are formulated better as short-answer questions.

B. *Short-Answer Questions*
- The question should be explicit enough to evoke the correct type of response.
- Failure should result *only* from lack of recall, not from an inability to understand the question because it is worded poorly or ambiguously.
- Construct the questions to allow objectivity of marking.
  Example: "What happened in 1776?" is less likely to elicit a circumscribed response than "What major event in U.S. history occurred in 1776?"

Major Strengths
- A rapid survey of information is possible.
- A large area of curriculum content can be covered.
- Student responses are relatively easy to mark.

Major Weaknesses

- It can be difficult to construct items that call for only one correct answer. (Too many cues may result in too many right answers, and too few cues may result in a variety of acceptable answers.)
- This type of test stresses rote recall and, if used exclusively, may encourage memorization without understanding.

Structured Response Tests　There are also a number of hints that can help in the construction of structured response items (matching, true-false, multiple choice).

A. *Matching*
- Matching items are appropriate means of testing for correct associations between related classes of information, such as inventors and inventions, major events and dates, products and the locations where they are produced, important people and the reasons for their importance, composers and compositions, and so on.

    Example: For each of the compositions on the right, select the composer (from left-hand column) who wrote it. Indicate your selections by placing the composer's name in the blank preceding his composition.

    Bach
    Beethoven　——Firebird Suite
    Brahms　　 ——Lullaby
    Chopin　　 ——None But the Lonely Heart
    Handel　　 ——Moonlight Sonata
    Mozart　　 ——The Water Music
    Stravinsky　——Don Juan
    Tchaikovsky ——Joy of My Soul
    Wagner

- Do not include too many items—ten to twelve maximum. If you include more, students will spend too much time hunting through the items.

- There should be more items in the "to be selected from" column than in the "matched to" column in order to reduce success from the process of elimination.
- Select material from one subject field only. Items should be from the same class, and all choices should be plausible from the cues given.
  Example: Avoid choices like:

bulbs	——relativity
Einstein	—— an export of Holland
Seasons are determined by —— Depression
1930s	——theaters
plays	——the tilt of the earth in relation to the sun

- Arrange names in alphabetical order and dates in chronological order.
- Instructions must be *clear*. Some statement must clearly indicate the purpose of the matching. For example, "Each city on the left is a capital of one of the NATO countries on the right."
- Keep questions on one page to avoid frustrating students with having to flip sheets constantly or turn pages.

Major Strengths
- These are compact items that can test a great deal of factual information in little space.
- Matching items allow for a rapid survey of specific events, people, definitions, and the like.

Major Weaknesses
- Matching items are very limited in the kinds of information and knowledge they can probe.

B. *True and False*
  - Attempt to keep a fifty-fifty balance between true (T) and false (F) statements.

- Avoid opinionated, trivial, or trick items.

  Example: T or F 1. Personality is more important than appearance.

  T or F 2. The ABC test of vocational aptitude contains 82 items arranged in nine sets.

- Avoid statements that are partly true and partly false, ambiguous, negative, and double negative.

  Example: 1. Lester Pearson was a great Canadian patriot and was prime minister of Canada.

  2. Not every teacher is careful to avoid having a student dislike his subject.

  3. Toronto is not the capital of Canada.

  4. Not all defense mechanisms are maladaptive.

- Avoid specific determiners. Items that contain words such as "all," "none," "always," or "never" tend to be false.

  Example: Corporal punishment is never justified.

Major Strengths

- Items can be scored easily and objectively.
- Items are relatively easy to construct.
- True-False tests take little time and can be used for frequent testing.
- Directions to true-false items are understood easily.

Major Weaknesses

- Items can be ambiguous or simplistic because statements are seldom totally true or totally false.
- Scores are subject to guessing and chance effects.
- If used exclusively or extensively, true-false tests may overemphasize rote memorization.

C. *Multiple Choice (Best Answer)*

- Basic construction involves the provision of a stem and from four to six choices. Only one choice is correct.

Example: The person most responsible for the current popularity of Adlerian psychology in the schools is:

1. William Glasser
2. Rudolph Dreikurs
3. Carl Rogers
4. B.F. Skinner
5. Albert Bandura
6. John Holt

- Increasing the homogeneity of choices generally increases the difficulty of the item.
- Choices should be equally plausible and grammatically homogeneous.

Example: Avoid statements like:

The person responsible for designing buildings is called *an*:

1. painter
2. pianist
3. professional athlete
4. architect
5. comedian

- Distribute the order of correct answers randomly and equally (avoid the temptation to favor first and last choices).
- Avoid divided stems.

Example: Percentile rank shows the percentage of subjects

1. at or below
2. above
3. right on
4. under
5. at and below the given score.

- Avoid cuing correct responses by making the correct choice longer or more consistent grammatically with the stem than other choices. The preceding example also illustrates this common error.

- Avoid the excessive use of negatively stated items. These can tend to be a bit more ambiguous than positively stated items.
- If "all of the above" and "none of the above" are used, they should be correct no more or less frequently than other choices.
- Check the pattern of correct choices throughout items to determine whether there is inadvertent patterning of correct answers—e.g., a, b, c, d, a, b, c, d, and so on.
- Each item should test independent information that gives no clues to the other items in the test.

Major Strengths
- These items can test for fairly fine discriminations in students' knowledge of important curriculum content.
- Like all structured response items, multiple-choice items may be scored objectively.

Major Weaknesses
- Good multiple-choice items are difficult and time consuming to construct.
- Multiple-choice items, like all structured response items, do not permit independent articulation of information in a student's own words.

Scoring and Grading

When a teacher has prepared the items that will make up the test, he or she should write a set of instructions for taking the test. The form the answers should take must be specified, and the criteria by which they will be judged (together with the system of scoring) should be indicated clearly. If this process is neglected, the teacher does not have a basis for fair and valid scoring of pupil responses.

The rule of thumb here is that both teacher and pupil should be entirely knowledgeable about scoring procedures (i.e., procedures for assigning quantitative values to the quality of pupil responses).

An *answer guide* is a sensible aid for scoring tests. (Essay questions can be approached by jotting down the points you will be looking for in student answers.) Such guides help the marker avoid biases in scoring. Biases can also be reduced by letter-coding the different sections of a test, mixing them up, and scoring one section at a time. Scoring and grading should be done at different times. Both may be done several times, with the test papers in different sequences. All of these techniques reduce the likelihood of unwitting bias in scoring. The teacher should do anything possible to double-check the accuracy of the scoring procedure. A very good test of scoring/grading reliability is to give a sample of test papers, together with the list of scoring/grading procedures, to a colleague. If your scoring/grading procedures are clear and your use of them consistent, both you and your colleague should arrive at similar conclusions.

When you score pupil examinations, it is important to double-check the usefulness of each test item. The way pupils respond to an item can indicate whether it is a bad item and should be deleted. Whether test items are of the restricted or structured variety, it is possible for a teacher to determine the merit of a particular item by examining the responses to that item in comparison with responses to all other items in the test. If students who have answered most of the other questions correctly do not score well on a specific item, this may indicate that the question is ambiguous, confusing, or unfair. If, on the other hand, almost every student responds correctly to an item, it may be a poor item in that it doesn't subserve any discriminatory function. Many sophisticated statistical techniques are available to assist in such item analyses (Thorndike and Hagen, 1977), but the general principles are not difficult to grasp and apply in a less esoteric manner. Finally, tests should be returned to students as quickly as possible and should be accompanied by specific teacher comments. Such feedback is essential in order to optimize the learning potential in a test situation. *Remember that the primary aim of testing is to facilitate learning.*

EVALUATION OF INSTRUCTIONAL EFFECTIVENESS

There is an old joke about teacher attitudes that states that, when learners progress well, teachers are successful; but when learners don't progress well, it is the learners who fail. In other words, it is easy for most of us who teach to take credit for pupil success but much more difficult to take blame for pupil failure. The question of *instructional effectiveness* is really a question of what effects a teacher's instructional skills have on the academic and social progress of pupils. Do learners fail, or do teachers? Do teachers succeed, or do learners? The truth of the matter would seem to fall somewhere in the middle. Since teaching and learning are completely interfaced, it is only reasonable to assume that both teachers and pupils play an important part in success and failure. It is the quality of the interchange between teachers and learners that is most responsible for educational successes or failures.

Instructional effectiveness research is a branch of educational research that attempts to link different kinds of instructional actions (skills, strategies, styles) to student learning behaviors in classrooms, to student learning of subject matter (achievement), and to students' attitudes toward instruction. Such research has attempted to determine whether certain teaching methods produce greater academic gains than other methods. Will certain instructional skills increase pupil learning when employed by a wide variety of teachers? The major aim of instructional effectiveness research has been to discover specific instructional skills that are consistently related to pupil achievement. Such information is required in order to improve teacher training programs and the quality of classroom instruction that is affected by such training.

Unfortunately, recent surveys of instructional effectiveness research (e.g., Brophy and Evertson, 1976; Dunkin and Biddle, 1974) seem to agree that, to date, efforts to relate instructional behaviors to student learning and achievement causally have been disappointing, inconclusive, and often unproductive. It would seem that, while many of us (laypeople, teachers, administrators, university professors) believe that we can spot good teaching when we see it, effective instruction is extremely elusive. Effective instruction would seem not to be a matter of good form alone. In other words, although a teacher may do all of the actions we think teachers should do, they may or may not facilitate effective pupil learning. There is a wealth of evidence that indicates that an understanding of instructional effectiveness cannot be approached through generalizations about what all teachers should do regardless of instructional setting, pupil characteristics, or specific differences in subject matter. The model of instructional effectiveness presented here is based on an integrated awareness of both context-specific instructional objectives and instructional skills that are congruent with these objectives. In this model, a balance between instructional behaviors and instructional cognitions is basic to effective pedagogy.

A Functional Definition of Instructional Effectiveness

Regardless of what effective instruction should look like, it is still possible to say that effective instruction creates learning performances that meet reasonable instructional objectives. Notice that this definition is *functional* as opposed to *structural*. Nowhere in the definition is there a description of what specific teaching actions make up effective instruction (i.e., a *structure*). Rather, the definition views effective instruction as a process (*function*) that underlies successful learning performances. This means that effective instruction may take on a great variety of forms or structures but always must have the function of producing demonstrable learning gains in relation to instructional objectives. Presumably, if a teacher's selection of interactive teaching skills is appropriate to his or her instructional objective, that teacher has a good chance of being effective. Thus, the actual skills and strategies a teacher employs could be very different for each instructional objective, situation, and grade level. Yet all these different methods could be considered effective as long as they promote the intended (and stated) pupil learning.

Viewing instructional effectiveness from a functional perspective is of tremendous assistance in analyzing the effectiveness of an individual teacher in a particular classroom with a particular group of pupils. There are two questions that must be answered to permit such an analysis: (1) Are pupils' learning performances changing in accordance with specific instructional objectives? (2) Are the instructional skills and strategies selected by the teacher appropriate to the instructional objectives? If so, is the teacher actually performing these skills and strategies? Thus, to analyze instructional effectiveness in individual cases, you must have a clear understanding of the specific instructional objectives being approached, the learning progress of pupils, and the intended and actual interactive skills employed. Such evaluation requires that pupil learning be assessed reliably and validly, and that interactive instructional skills be analyzed in relation to pupil learning. The model of formative evaluation discussed in the following section incorporates an evaluation of pupil learning and an analysis of interactive instructional skills to produce a very practical method of evaluating instructional effectiveness.

Formative Evaluation of Teaching Effectiveness

Since an evaluation of instructional effectiveness must include both an evaluation of pupil learning and an analysis of interactive instructional skills, such evaluations must always be undertaken with a clear understanding of specific instructional objectives and intended teacher actions. The evaluator and the classroom teacher must work together very closely. (The necessity for close collaboration actually makes this system of evaluation an excellent method for teacher self-analysis. More will be said about this unique advantage throughout this section.) The formative model for evaluation also assumes that whatever information is gained concerning current instructional effectiveness will be channelled into an ongoing program of teacher skill development. In this way, teachers improve their instructional efforts by making use of information about their effectiveness.

The formative model for evaluation is a theoretical and practical amalgam of clinical methods of supervision (Cogan, 1973; Goldhammer, 1969), analysis of interactive instructional skill, and systematic evaluation of pupil learning progress (Martin and Reed, 1977). The model consists of four distinct steps that recur in a cyclical manner. Figure 5.2 summarizes the major components of the formative evaluation model.

The *preteaching conference* is perhaps the most important com-

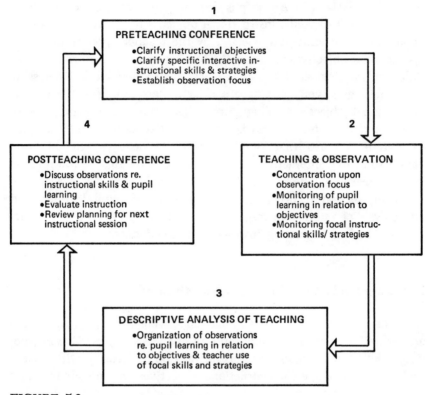

FIGURE 5.2

ponent in the formative evaluation system. What is established at this time largely determines subsequent observations and evaluations. The main purpose of the preteaching conference is to provide a clear focus for the evaluation of instruction. This is done by (1) clearly stating instructional objectives in terms of observable learner performances, and (2) clearly defining the most important instructional skills and strategies to be employed in facilitating learner performances. If a teacher is working with a colleague, supervisor, or even pupils, clarification of objectives and skills can be accomplished through focused discussion. If a teacher is working alone, the preteaching activities take place in personal thoughts and reflections. In either setting, the objectives and instructional skills highlighted during the preconference should be written down for future reference.

Before the preteaching conference ends, some method should be determined for observing and recording the teacher's use of the focal interactive skills selected. Try not to focus on more than two or three important and appropriate skills at any one time.

In most instances it is enough for the observer (supervisor or colleague) simply to note each occurrence of the focal skills (and perhaps to note a bit of what happens immediately before and after use of each skill). When working alone, teachers must try to store similar information mentally while they are teaching. Both kinds of observation demand considerable skill and are difficult at first. Fortunately, with some practice these observation skills are not too difficult to master (particularly if the focus of observation is restricted to two or three key skills). The important thing to remember about the preconference is that, at the end of it, the teacher should have a clear understanding of instructional objectives and specific interactive instructional skills. When an external observer is present, it is essential that both teacher and observer share such understandings. (Learning and using the taxonomy of skills described in Chapter 4 can help teacher and observer share a common language and understandings.)

After the preteaching conference, the instructional lesson occurs. During this period of interactive teaching and direct observation, attention is focused on (1) monitoring the learning performances of pupils in relation to the instructional objectives established in the preteaching conference, and (2) monitoring the focal instructional skills employed by the teacher. Such observations (and their recording) should always be done in the manner decided during the preteaching conference.

After the period of active instruction, the teacher and the observer should spend a brief period together. During this time they should organize their observations into precise descriptive accounts of what occurred. Were the instructional objectives met? Were the focal instructional skills actually used? Did the instructional skills used seem to help learners meet the instructional objectives? All of these questions should be answerable from the descriptive accounts produced from the observational records. In framing answers to such questions, it is important to avoid *inferences* and *value judgments*. The focus should always be limited to a straightforward *descriptive analysis* of what actually happened without inferences about why it happened or whether what happened was good or bad. Premature inferences and value judgments most often prevent the development of a clear descriptive record.

When teachers are working alone to evaluate their instructional effectiveness, the descriptive analysis phase moves automatically into a *postteaching conference*. When an external observer is available, teacher and observer must now come together for this final phase in the formative evaluation model. During the postteaching conference, descriptive analyses of learning outcomes and instructional skills are exchanged, discussed, and scrutinized. Like any good feedback session, the tone of the postteaching conference should be positive, encouraging, and specific. Vague communications, inferences, and value judgments should be avoided. The focus should be confined to the areas described in the preteaching conference. Were the specific instructional objectives met? Were the focal instructional skills employed? If both questions can be answered affirmatively, and if the skills used can be connected logically to the learning outcomes attained, it is likely that the instruction was effective. If the answers to the questions are not affirmative, it is important to double-check the appropriateness of the instructional objectives and the interactive instructional skills. If the objectives prove to be stated clearly and to be in line with pupil entry capabilities (see Chapter 3) and if the focal instructional skills still seem to be appropriate means of facilitating learning performances, the teacher should use the feedback offered during the postteaching conference to structure another attempt to teach the same lesson.

It is important to realize that the formative evaluation model should operate in an *ongoing* manner to assist teachers in constantly monitoring their instructional effectiveness. In this way, one lesson's postteaching conference can lead naturally into another lesson's preteaching conference. This provides continual opportunity for conscious skill development and growth. Initial attempts to impose the kind of foci advocated by the formative model may be time consuming and require the assistance of an external observer. Fortunately, it is possible (with practice) for this formative system to become largely internalized as standard, habitual preparation and reflection that the individual teacher can employ efficiently, with only occasional outside assistance.

An illustration of the application of the formative evaluation model to the practical evaluation and development of instructional skills is provided by the experiences of Edward, an eleventh-grade social studies teacher. Toward the end of his first year as a regular classroom discussions in a calm, logical fashion." After attempting his seeming inability to achieve what he thought to be an essential instructional objective. In its general form, this objective was that "students will learn to express their opinions to each other during classroom discussions in a calm, logical fashion." After attempting several group discussion lessons toward this objective, Edward became angry and discouraged about the lack of progress his students were making. Very seldom did any pupil directly express an opinion to another pupil. Even when this rare event did occur, it usually ended right there, with no response by other pupils to the opinion expressed.

In recent weeks, Edward had been attempting to employ redirection skills of *peer involvement* (see the skill taxonomy in Chapter 4) to encourage attainment of the instructional objective. In order to assist him in acquiring this new skill, he asked a more experienced colleague (Roberta) to observe one of his lessons. After first determining exactly what the objective was and the kind of student-to-student exchange that would indicate its accomplishment, Edward and Roberta discussed the specific skill of peer involvement. Edward described the skill and gave some examples of it (e.g., "O.K., Sam, I noticed you frowning while Sandra said that. What were you disagreeing with?" or "What's your reaction to that, Jurri?"). Together, he and Roberta developed a method that Roberta could use to record each time Edward used the skill. They also agreed that Roberta would record what occurred after each use of the skill. When the preparation had been done, Edward taught the lesson and Roberta observed it. She recorded meticulously each instance of redirection for peer involvement. After some independent reflection about what had occurred, Roberta and Edward met to discuss the lesson. Two things were immediately obvious: (1) students did not engage in very much pupil-to-pupil expression of opinions, and (2) Edward, even though he thought he was using the peer involvement skill, only used it once in the entire forty-five-minute period. The second point came as a surprise to Edward. He gradually began to realize that his anxiety about performing the new skill had led him to think so much about it that it seemed like he was using it when he really was not. With this new insight, Edward planned a number of general forms for using the peer involvement skill in future lessons. He practiced and thought about these forms of the skill at various times over the weekend. When he next taught a lesson that attempted to reach the objective of pupil-to-pupil opinion exchange, he was delighted with the way in which he was able to use the skill. When actually used, the skill encouraged pupils to respond actively to each other's expressed opinions.

The foregoing illustration provides a practical example of use of the formative model for evaluation of instructional effectiveness (Fig. 5.2) and development of interactive instructional skills. As the example shows, the various phases of this model do not need to be implemented in a formalistic manner in order to be effective. The most important result of employing such a system is that it forces teachers to focus on specific aspects of their interactive skills that are intended to result in the student learning performances stated in instructional objectives. Once this focus has been attained, the model can be employed in a variety of ways to yield useful, informational feedback about a teacher's classroom use of interactive skills.

The formative evaluation model is concerned primarily with providing an opportunity for the evaluation and development of effective interactive instructional skills in a realistic, relaxed atmosphere. Such skill development is an excellent way to increase professional expertise and confidence while simultaneously decreasing unproductive stress and worry.

Before leaving this section, it is necessary to make an important distinction between *effective* teaching and *good* teaching. While ineffective teaching can never be considered good teaching, effective teaching does not guarantee good teaching. Good teaching must be effective in an ethical and humane manner. While it is possible to teach effectively through the use of inhumane, barbaric instructional practices, such teaching is always to be abhorred. Individual teachers are responsible for being thoroughly familiar with the ethical standards of the teaching association(s) to which they belong, and for developing and maintaining high professional standards with respect to basic human rights and liberties in the classroom. Use of the term *effective instruction* in this chapter assumes that practicing teachers are capable of making sound ethical discriminations with respect to their instructional practices.

QUESTIONS AND RESPONSES

1. *Q:* It still seems to me that the whole concept of grading or evaluating someone is counterproductive to learning and development.

   R: This chapter has talked about the differences between evaluating pupil learning for purposes of classification and evaluating pupil learning for purposes of feedback and diagnosis. When evaluation is primarily for feedback purposes and occurs relatively frequently in a variety of forms (e.g., oral questioning, written quizzes, laboratory write-ups, skilled performance demonstrations, etc.), it can be integrated smoothly into learning and development processes. When this happens, it is difficult to know where learning ends and evaluation begins. In such cases, evaluation simply becomes a part of the entire learning process. Remember too, that it is the learning *performances* that are evaluated, not the individual pupils. A pupil as a person should always be respected and nurtured. This does not mean, however, that pupils should not receive evaluative feedback about some of the things they do. It is every teacher's responsibility to make it clear to pupils that, while they may at times do things that are incorrect, wrong, or mistaken, they themselves are never incorrect, wrong, or mistaken. It also is important to remember that pupils learn more from evaluative feedback that emphasizes things they have done well rather than that which picks out every single mistake and totally ignores correct or promising performances.

2. *Q:* Some of the statements in this chapter seem to indicate that, when pupils fail, the teacher is probably being ineffective. Aren't certain kids just basically incapable of learning?

R: Obviously, learners are different in terms of what they can do and can't do. At one time it was popular to ascribe such differences to basic variations in intelligence, learning capacity, or academic aptitude. Over the past few decades, however, there has been an increasing amount of evidence to indicate that well-conceived instructional programs (e.g., the Head Start and Follow-Through programs in the United States) can alter pupils' intelligence quotients (IQs) dramatically. Such research shows clearly that constructs like IQ are not basic characteristics of a person that cannot be affected by learning and development. On the contrary, many of these constructs are understood best as measures of current general levels of learning.

The point here is that, while pupils in a given classroom may represent wide differences in acquired skills and knowledge, all pupils are first and foremost *potential learners* and should be treated as such. It is a teacher's responsibility to gauge each pupil's entry capabilities accurately (see Chapter 3) and to set instructional objectives for each pupil's learning that are in line with these capabilities. Large differences in pupil entry behavior may mean that pupils will learn different amounts and will reach different levels of broad curriculum goals. It definitely should not mean that some pupils will learn nothing. If this happens, then ineffective teaching is clearly indicated. Remember that effective teaching is always related to the promotion of learning in accordance with reasonable instructional objectives (i.e., objectives that are within the grasp of each pupil on the basis of his or her unique capabilities).

3. *Q:* You say that it is impossible to recognize effective instruction just by watching someone teach and without knowing what the objectives for that lesson are. I disagree. Certain teachers obviously are excited, enthusiastic, and competent; others are not. You don't have to be too sharp to see these differences.

R: I agree that some teachers are more appealing than others, and that we all can determine which teachers we might like more than others. However, I think that it is important not to confuse "appeal" or "behavior resembling our image of an ideal teacher" with instructional effectiveness. Teachers may be effective in many different ways, and it is not always the case that the stereotypic bright, lively, enthusiastic teacher accomplishes all the tasks of an effective teacher. Research on teaching (see Dunkin and Biddle, 1974) has failed consistently to correlate interactive instructional skills and styles with positive pupil learning and instructionally relevant attitudes across the board. Again, instructional effectiveness is achieved and measured by teacher behavior that is appropriate to facilitation of pupil learning in relation to instructional objectives. What may be effective for one teacher may not be effective for another. Gauging instructional effectiveness is not simply a matter of rating teacher enthusiasm, niceness, or organization. The real question is, "Are any of these actions effective for the pupils in a specific classroom in terms of instructional objectives X, Y, and Z?" The formative system for reevaluating instructional effectiveness presented in this chapter is one attempt to assist teachers in gauging their effectiveness in order to answer this question.

4. *Q:* How can I get feedback about my own instructional effectiveness?

R: The formative evaluation system discussed in this chapter is about the best way I know to structure such feedback. When you first use this system, encourage colleagues, friends, and perhaps certain pupils to observe some of your teaching actions. Audiotapes and videotapes of classroom sessions can allow you to observe yourself in a less hectic manner than trying to observe yourself in the act of teaching. Whatever system of feedback you employ, remember to consider your own skill performance in light of whether or not pupils actually learned anything. An ongoing system of valid and reliable evaluation of pupil learning is a prerequisite for any analysis of your instructional effectiveness. In each lesson, you must arrange opportunities for students to demonstrate what they have learned (by question-and-answer, activity participation, formal quiz, group discussion, etc.). Once you have determined whether learning has occurred, you are in a position to examine carefully the specific instructional skills and strategies you used to promote such learning. In short, feedback about your instructional effectiveness is obtained from a combination of careful evaluations of pupil learning and an analysis of actual instructional performance—from direct personal observation, videotape or audiotape reproduction, direct external observation, or whatever other means you can employ.

SUGGESTED ACTIVITIES

1. Develop systems for evaluating pupil learning for the instructional objectives you wrote in the Suggested Activities section of Chapter 3. How will you test for the learning performances indicated in the objectives? How will you make sure your evaluation systems are valid and reliable?

2. Write out some specific test items that you might use in a formal teacher-made classroom test for some of the learning performances considered in the first activity. Write some items that require structured responses, some that require restricted responses, and some that require essay responses.

3. How would you explain the evaluation systems developed in activity one to pupils? How would you make it clear that the evaluation systems were intended to be helpful and to facilitate pupil learning? Write down the exact words you would use to convey this message.

4. Reteach the short lessons you developed in Chapter 4, either to pupils in a classroom or to a group of your peers. Arrange for a friend or colleague to implement the formative evaluation model to examine your instructional effectiveness. Make certain that both instructional objectives and skill foci are discussed during the preteaching conference. Exchange roles after a few practice lessons, and act as observer while your friend or colleague teaches the same

or a different lesson. Make sure to restrict your postteaching discussions to descriptive accounts of what occurred, and avoid premature inferences and value judgments about what occurred.

REFERENCES

Brophy, J.E., and Evertson, C.M. 1976. *Learning from Teaching.* Boston: Allyn and Bacon.

Buros, O. 1972. *The Seventh Mental Measurements Yearbook.* Highland Park, N.J.: Gryphon Press.

Cogan, M.L. 1973. *Clinical Supervision.* Boston: Houghton Mifflin.

Dunkin, M., and Biddle, B. 1974. *The Study of Teaching.* New York: Holt, Rinehart and Winston.

Goldhammer, R. 1969. *Clinical Supervision.* New York: Holt, Rinehart and Winston.

Grunland, N.E. 1976. *Measurement and Evaluation in Teaching.* New York: Macmillan.

Martin, J., and Reed, M. 1977. Formative Evaluation: the Simon Fraser Model." *Challenge* 16: 16–20.

Thorndike, R.L., and Hagen, E.P. 1977. *Measurement and Evaluation in Psychology and Education.* New York: John Wiley and Sons.

6

Total Instructional Planning

The final chapter of *Mastering Instruction* pulls together most of the information contained in previous chapters concerning what and how teachers think about what they do (*instructional cognitions*) and what they actually do (*instructional behaviors*). As stated in Chapter 1, the rationale for a joint emphasis on instructional cognitions and behaviors is that personal cognitions and behaviors have a direct role in determining professional effectiveness and thereby in reducing professional stress. These factors are more directly controllable by individual teachers than are external, situational factors; when they are controlled in a positive, productive manner, they influence situational factors in equally positive ways (Bandura, 1978). The teacher who is equipped with general cognitive beliefs and self-talk strategies to manage professional stress (see Chapter 1), and who combines a clear understanding of specific instructional processes and behaviors with an ability to perform critical preactive, interactive, and evaluative behaviors, is in a powerful position to plan and execute total instructional experiences. Such experiences should always result in significant pupil learning.

Most literature that deals with teaching or instruction begins with a discussion of instructional planning. This book does not discuss details of instructional planning until the final chapter. The positioning of this material is deliberate. It reflects the central notion that *total instructional planning is a dynamic, active process of instructional organization and preparation that demands complete comprehension of preactive, interactive, and evaluation behaviors and their interrelationships.* The central purpose of total instructional planning is promotion of effective and harmonious interplay among all the instructional cognitions and behaviors discussed thus far. Because of its far-reaching executive role, total instructional planning cannot be conceived properly until all the relevant instructional variables have been examined thoroughly (Cohen and Manion, 1977). In a proper plan, instructional objectives for a lesson are associated logically and creatively with interactive instructional skills and strategies to ensure that students will receive ample opportunity for meaningful practice of learning performances. Such pupil performances result in immediate, formative feedback that can be used to evaluate pupil learning and instructor effectiveness.

COMPONENTS OF INSTRUCTIONAL PLANS

A total plan for any instructional session should contain a clear, succinct statement of each of the following generic instructional elements:

1. A list of relevant *pupil entry capabilities* (including methods of preassessment, if necessary).
2. A short list of *instructional objectives* for the lesson (stated in a pupil-centered manner that clearly specifies intended learning performances).

3. A logical sequence of *lesson activities* together with a list of *interactive instructional skills and strategies* to be used at each stage. (A description of *curriculum materials* should be included with this sequence.)
4. A statement that indicates how the proposed activity sequence and instructional skills and strategies will help to guarantee that the lesson will make effective use of the basic learning principles of *meaningfulness, activity, feedback,* and *organization.*
5. A brief description of methods used to *evaluate pupil learning and instructional effectiveness.*

The successful incorporation of these five elements into any instructional plan can help teachers to structure their teaching preparations and force them to attend to important dimensions of curriculum materials, pupil behavior, instructional behavior, and their interrelationships. Perhaps the best way to demonstrate the total instructional planning process is to include a couple of specific lesson plans that incorporate the foregoing features. The first example (Lesson A) is appropriate for a grade four language arts class. The second example (Lesson B) is for a grade nine or ten social studies lesson.

Lesson A

(This lesson is based on some materials developed by Pamela Straker through the NITEP Student Teaching Project at the University of British Columbia, 1979.) *

---

* The central idea and many of the activities of this lesson are presented here with the kind permission of the Native Indian Teacher Education Program, University of British Columbia.

Subject: Language Arts   Grade: 4
Topic: Quotation Marks   Time: 40 minutes

I. *Pupil Entry Capabilities*
    All pupils must be able to do the following things in order to
    accomplish the instructional objectives of the lesson as a result
    of engaging in the instructional activities described below:

    1. Follow simple directions given orally by the teacher.
    2. Read aloud and silently at a rate of at least one word per
        second.
    3. Comprehend what is read (comprehension of vocabulary ap-
        propriate to the general grade three curriculum).
    4. Write phrases that have been read or spoken.
    5. Speak to teacher or classmates in an audible voice.

    Preassessment of entry capabilities is based on:
    1. Close individual observation of each pupil's reading, listening,
        writing, and speaking skills during previous language arts
        lessons.
    2. Pupil performances on specific reading, writing, and compre-
        hension exercises that have been given in the immediately
        preceding lesson. All exercises employed a vocabulary level
        similar to the level used in this lesson.

II. *Instructional Objectives*
    1. When reading, pupils will distinguish between narrative and
        spoken words on the basis of quotation marks.
    2. Pupils will write at least five direct quotes (with quotation
        marks properly placed) and will vary the placement of the
        speaker's name from one quote to the next.

III.

Lesson Activities	*Curric-ulum Materials*	*Important Interactive Instructional Skills and Strategies*
		Overall Strategy: Traditional Recitation and Seatwork Practice
Introduction		*Skills:*
1. Teacher shows example of a Q.D. (Quotation Detective) badge.	Q.D. badges (enough for all pupils)	Inducing Set
2. Explains that today pupils are going to be detectives. What they are looking for will be the exact words spoken by someone. Later they each will be given a badge and assignment to be a Q.D.	e.g., Q.D.	Overview and Statement of Objectives Transition
3. For the first group exercise, have pupils open a reader at any page and say, "Find an example of the exact words spoken by someone in the story." Call on pupils to read the spoken words and then state who was speaking. (Model the desired pupil response yourself to clarify the task if necessary.)	Grade four readers	Group Alerting Cues Showing Work Providing a Model
4. Ask what signs or signals are used to show the exact words spoken. Illustrate the correct	Chalk-board	Prompting Question

Lesson Activities	Curric- ulum Materials	Important Interactive Instructional Skills and Strategies
form of quotation marks (" and "—sixty-six and ninety-nine), and write the words "quotation marks" and their symbols on the board.		Markers of Importance

Development

1. To clarify the idea that quotation marks are placed around direct speech (only the exact words spoken), have a pupil say something while another pupil records his or her words on the board. Example: "Today's a very rainy day," said Irene. Repeat the activity with other children several times.

2. Illustrate the fact that the position of the speaker's name may be varied. Draw attention to examples such as:
   (a) *Sue* said, "This isn't mine, it's yours."
   (b) "This isn't mine, it's yours," *said Sue.*
   (c) "This isn't mine," *said Sue,* "it's yours."
   Have pupils find examples in their readers.

3. Direct attention to the following boardwork:
   "_____," said _____.
   "_____?" asked _____.

Right column entries aligned with activities:

Transition

Incorporating Pupil Response

Redirecting

Verbal Markers of Importance

Fact Recall Questioning Redirecting Post-Question Wait Time

Transition

Lesson Activities	*Curriculum Materials*	*Important Interactive Instructional Skills and Strategies*
"_____!" exclaimed _____. _____ said "_____." _____ asked, "_____?" _____ exclaimed, "_____!" Have pupils fill in the blanks orally, and assign a second set of examples for pupils to write down in their notebooks.	Notebooks	Conceptual Questioning Redirecting Peer Involvement Descriptive Praise Random Recitation
4. Have pupils transcribe the following sentences in their notebooks, placing quotation marks correctly:		Transition
Jenny said, I enjoyed this story.		Informational Feedback
It's late, said Bob, and I'm going home.		Post-Response Wait Time
Where have you been? asked Jill.		
Observe pupil responses and note individual difficulties. Correct orally.		Incorporating Pupil Response

Conclusion

1. Review when and how quotation marks are used.   Lesson Review

2. Distribute Q.D. badges for each pupil to wear.   Descriptive Praise

3. Assign follow-up homework to be checked tomorrow.   Transition
    "As a Quotation Detective you are to write down at least five direct quotes you hear today. Be sure to use your

Lesson Activities	Curric- ulum Materials	Important Interactive Instructional Skills and Strategies
quotation marks correctly each time. Vary the position of speakers' names from one quote to the next." (Illustrate desired task through modeling.)		Modeling for Self-Evaluation

IV. *Learning Principles Used*
   (a) *Meaningfulness* is enhanced by creation of a small game situation through the Q.D. badges and by relation of the concept of quotation marks to direct quotes in pupils' own experiences in and out of school.
   (b) *Activity* is provided in the form of appropriate seatwork, oral responses, and reading and searching activities that are related directly to the learning performances stated in the instructional objectives.
   (c) *Feedback* is provided immediately and positively through descriptive praise and informational feedback about seatwork and oral recitation.
   (d) *Organization* seems logical in that the lesson activities build on the skills developed in preceding activities.

V. *Evaluation*
   (a) *Pupil Learning.* Pupils' use of quotation marks to distinguish between narrative and spoken words is demonstrated in the last part of the introduction and in the second part of the development phases of the lesson. While marking and grading are not done formally at these times, the teacher can observe which children are and are not responding accurately (particularly if random recitation ensures that all pupils have at least one opportunity to participate).

   The homework assignment tests directly for the learning performances in the second objective. The assignment could be marked and graded as part of the overall course assessment of each pupil's performance in language arts.

(b) *Instructional Effectiveness.* It should be easy to ascertain the extent to which objectives have been met. In addition, the specific use of precise instructional skills will be monitored by an outside observer (a colleague) and by the teacher, who will adopt a formative evaluation strategy. The relation between skill use and facilitation of learning performances will be examined.

Lesson B

Subject: Social Studies   Grade: 9/10
Topic: Democracy   Time: 90 minutes

I. *Pupil Entry Capabilities*
This lesson is intended as an initial lesson to provide the teacher with indications about learners'

1. current understandings of abstract sociopolitical concepts;
2. ability to express their ideas orally and in writing;
3. ability to engage in basic conceptual and analytic reasoning; and
4. ability to work cooperatively and productively in seatwork and small-group and large-group recitation settings.

Thus, the lesson is largely for purposes of preassessment. The only entry capabilities assumed are general writing, reading, speaking, and listening skills basic to any junior high school curriculum.

II. *Instructional Objectives*
1. Learners will develop conceptual definitions of the term *democracy* by engaging in a concept attainment process that requires pupils gradually to induce abstract concepts from basic concrete exemplars or instances of the concept.
2. In working toward objective (1), pupils will demonstrate the various academic capabilities and skills discussed in the section on pupil entry capabilities.

III.

Lesson Activities	Curric- ulum Materials	Important Interactive Instructional Skills and Strategies
		Overall Strategy: ConceptAttainment (different type of strategy from the basic concept attainment strategy described in Chapter 4)
		Skills:
1. Teacher states objective (1) and passes out index cards so that each pupil has a pile of 25–50 cards.	Index cards (mini- mum of 25 per pupil)	Statement of Objectives
2. Teacher explains that the term *democracy* can mean many things, and asks pupils to think about democracy. Every time a pupil has a single thought or idea about democracy, he or she is to write it on an index card. Teacher demonstrates this by thinking out loud and writing one or two ideas on index cards. Give pupils ten minutes for this task.		Group Alerting Cues Verbal Markers of Importance Modeling Statement of Transition
3. Pupils write ideas on cards. Teacher circulates and encourages.		Goal-Directed Prompts Prompting Questions Descriptive Praise

Lesson Activities	Curric- ulum Materials	Important Interactive Instructional Skills and Strategies
		Informational Feedback Showing Work
4. Teacher asks pupils to stop writing down ideas and asks them to sort their cards into various piles, putting to- gether cards that "just seem to go together." Teacher asks pupils to sort without trying to give them- selves exact reasons for put- ting each card into a par- ticular pile (five minutes are allotted for this task).		Statement of Transition Group Alerting Cues Verbal Markers of Importance Statement of Transition
5. Teacher gives instructions to examine each pile of cards they have formed and to write a simple word or phrase on another card that seems to describe best the idea common to all of the cards in any given pile (five minutes are allotted for this task).		Statement of Transition Group Alerting Cues Statement of Transition
6. Teacher requests that pupils examine their pile-label cards very carefully and write down a definition of democracy formed from arranging the words and phrases on their pile-label		Statement of Transition Group Alerting Cues Goal-Directed

Lesson Activities	Curric- ulum Materials	Important Interactive Instructional Skills and Strategies
cards into a sentence that begins with the words "Democracy is . . ." (five minutes are allotted for this task).		Prompt Statement of Transition
7. Teacher directs pupils to divide themselves into groups of four or five to discuss their pile-label cards and definitions. Each group is asked to appoint a recorder who will write down common labels and definitional elements. Each group will generate a group definition of democracy by stringing together these common elements (thirty minutes are allotted for this task).		Overview Overview Group Alerting Cues
Teacher moves from group to group to ensure that each pupil has an opportunity to participate actively.		Redirecting Promoting Peer Involvement
8. Teacher directs pupils back to their regular places. Asks group recorders for each group's definition and records these on the chalkboard.	Chalk-board; chalk	Statement of Transition Physical Arrangement Incorporating Pupil Responses Showing Work
9. Teacher leads a large group recitation during which		Random Recitation Redirecting

Lesson Activities	Curriculum Materials	Important Interactive Instructional Skills and Strategies
pupils are asked to compare and give opinions about the various group definitions. Through focused questioning, teacher assists pupils in forming a final class definition of the term *democracy* (no more than 20 minutes are allotted for this activity.)		Peer Involvement Conceptual Questioning Opining Questions Judgmental Questions Incorporating Pupil Responses
10. Teacher summarizes main points in the definition, describes the process of concept attainment the class has gone through, and expresses appreciation for pupils' hard work and clever ideas. Teacher also indicates how today's lesson will lead into the next social studies lesson.		Statement of Transition Lesson Review

Descriptive Praise

Curriculum Links |

IV. *Learning Principles Used*

The inductive process followed in this lesson provides ample opportunity for *meaningfulness* (pupils generate their own ideas before discussing them in small- and large-group settings); *activity* (all pupils active at desks, then in small groups, then in large group); *feedback* (teacher gives direct one-to-one feedback during seatwork, and other pupils and teacher give feedback about each pupil's ideas during small-group discussions); and *organization* (logical, inductive sequence).

V. *Evaluation*

The primary instructional objective is stated in a manner that permits the teacher to evaluate pupil learning progress infor-mally as the lesson moves along. Since each phase of the lesson is dependent on successful completion of the previous phase, the ability of the class to formulate a comprehensive definition of democracy provides clear demonstration of the attainment of the primary instructional objective. Teaching effectiveness will be examined in relation to the successful attainment of this objective. During transition periods the teacher will keep track of the teach-ing skills that are being used by checking off the interactive skills listed in the lesson plan. After the lesson is concluded, the teacher can review these skills and make notes about which skills were successful in moving the lesson along and which were not. Such notes can be invaluable resources for planning future les-sons for which similar strategies and instructional procedures would be appropriate.

EVERYDAY PLANNING

The sample lesson plans in the previous section provide comprehen-sive illustrations of the total instructional planning process and give attention to important aspects of preactive, interactive, and evalua-tion phases. However, the practical demands of everyday instructional life in schools make such detailed planning impossible in many in-stances. With little or no formal preparation time included in their job descriptions, most teachers must find time for proper instructional planning in their personal, after-hours time. Fortunately, proper in-structional preparation does not require a great deal of time (Popham and Baker, 1970) and does not always need to be reflected in the crea-tion of comprehensive plans such as those examined here.

Practical, everyday planning most often resembles a shorthand version of the elaborate, detailed plans in the preceding section. Short-hand plans do not leave out any of the crucial notions about pre-assessment, objectives, activities, skills and strategies, and evaluation. They permit teachers, after careful thought, to create a short list of instructional cues to which they can refer immediately before, during, and after the active instructional period defined in the plan. Learning to do this kind of planning is an important part of practical teaching and can reduce needless worry and anxiety about instruction. The investment of reasonable time and energy can give large returns in well-organized, effective instructional performances.

Probably the best way to acquire shorthand planning skills is to begin by producing a few elaborate instructional plans, such as the sample lesson plans presented earlier. This initial practice ensures that the teacher will comprehend and be able to consider all aspects of instructional preparation. The detailed planning of instructional skills and strategies is a particularly important part of this initially elaborate planning. Teachers should explore thoroughly skill and strategy taxonomies such as those presented in Chapter 4 in order to acquire a basic nomenclature for referencing aspects of interactive instructional behavior. The initial time devoted to this elaborate planning and to the acquisition of a strong cognitive repertoire of instructional actions is rewarded powerfully when instructors begin to reduce their instructional preparation time by adopting a variety of shorthand techniques. This is so because the initial expenditure of time and effort helps to ensure that really important planning components will not be omitted.

Over time, most teachers can refine their shorthand planning skills gradually to the point where they can prepare most lessons in five to ten minutes. This is particularly true if similar lesson structures and instructional skills have been used in previous lessons. Of course, each time a new strategy or novel activity sequence is attempted, teachers can expect preparation to be slightly more time consuming. As a rule, this does not prevent teachers from experimenting with new or altered instructional plans. The variety resulting from such experimentation can far outweigh the greater time required to prepare for it.

To illustrate the process of shorthand instructional planning, I have included the following version of Lesson B (presented earlier).

Democracy Lesson

(Need index cards and chalkboard)

1. Assume general writing, reading, etc., skills for junior high level.

2. Objectives: (a) Inductively create personal definitions of democracy.

(b) In doing (a), demonstrate key academic
skills.

Activities	*Key Instructional Actions*
Introduce: links, overview, and objectives.	—State objectives
Use inductive card sort to:	
1. create connotations—1/card	—Clear instructions
2. sort into piles	—Encourage with prompts,
3. label piles	praise, etc.
4. write definition— "Democracy is . . ."	—Make clear transitions
	—Review and links
5. discuss in groups and get group definition	
6. large group input—use recorders	
Summarize and link to next time.	

Evaluation

Pupils: Note individual and group performances in relation to
objectives.

Me: Focus on own use of transitions and links.

This abbreviated plan can be written on a single index card.
It takes little time to prepare and, for the teacher using it, cues all of
the essential components of total instructional planning. Of course,
shorthand preparation can be performed effectively only by teachers
who are well versed in the instructional cognitions and behaviors discussed throughout this book. Specific knowledge of these instructional
factors, together with the acquisition of more general strategies to cope
with instructional stress, can assist teachers in both planning and
executing effective instructional programs. By taking control of the
factors that help to determine their job satisfaction, instructional effectiveness, and ability to cope with professional stress, teachers can help
themselves master most instructional situations. To paraphrase Ban-

dura (1977), excellent performance in any field results when professionals use self-generated influences, in the form of personal cognitions and behaviors, to mount and sustain innovative efforts and superior accomplishments.

QUESTIONS AND RESPONSES

1. *Q:* This chapter has talked a lot about planning of individual lessons. What about planning entire courses or curriculum units?

R: The same skills required to do effective total lesson planning are used to plan courses or extended units of instruction. Unit plans should contain the following:

1. A list of relevant *pupil entry capabilities and preassessment procedures.* (If the lessons that make up a unit of instruction are sequenced logically so that each lesson builds on the learning performances of previous lessons, entry capabilities and preassessments may be considered most profitably with respect to the first lesson in the unit sequence.)
2. A list of *instructional objectives* for the entire unit. This list can be broken down or expanded to include specific instructional objectives for each lesson in the unit.
3. A logical sequence of *instructional activities, curriculum materials,* and *interactive instructional skills and strategies.* These can be broken down or expanded into specific lesson activities, materials, and skills/strategies.
4. A brief description of how *basic learning principles* are incorporated into the instructional design of the unit.
5. A description of *evaluation methods* for both learning and teaching. This can include copies of quizzes, tests, observational criteria, and the like. (Evaluation of pupil learning should receive systematic treatment in whole unit planning and should incorporate the principles of *reliability* and *validity,* as described in Chapter 5.)

When you do unit or course planning, you can begin by developing an overall outline of the entire unit or course in relation to the foregoing topics. You then can prepare a series of appropriate individual lesson plans. Individual lesson plans should be based on a more elaborate and specific expansion of the original unit outline. Always make sure that individual lessons are integrated fully into the overall unit outline.

2. *Q:* My lesson plans never turn out as I intend them. I think this is all right, because I believe that strict adherence to such plans destroys the important spontaneity of pupil learning. A teacher must always be flexible.

R: There is nothing wrong with planning a lesson and then *deciding* to abandon the plan as you are in the process of teaching. Lesson plans are not intended to be straitjackets. The key word here, however, is *deciding*. Teachers should always be aware of exactly what is occurring in their classes and how such activities relate to desirable learning outcomes. Teachers often encounter unplanned events in their classes that provide excellent opportunities for significant learning experiences. Good teachers recognize such opportunities and do not allow shortsighted adherence to a specific lesson plan to prevent them from pursuing such events. The main advantage of a lesson plan is that it provides a tool with which teachers can keep track of what has and has not occurred, what learnings have and have not taken place. When a teacher abandons part of a lesson plan (or the entire plan), this should be a *conscious decision* based on an accurate assessment of the instructional value of the unplanned event as compared with planned events. Although classroom events may occur spontaneously, the resultant teacher responses and decisions should never be capricious. Informed and accountable flexibility is a strong instructional asset. Careless, irresponsible flexibility, on the other hand, is a definite instructional liability.

Although flexibility can be an asset, deviations from lesson plans probably should not be so frequent and complete as to render lesson planning a meaningless activity. If your lesson plans never "come out right," it is likely that you are not executing your planning properly. Any number of things may be the cause, but I would suggest the following:

1. Make sure that your pupils' entry capabilities are appropriate to the instructional objectives and activities of the lessons.
2. Make sure that your own selection and execution of interactive instructional skills are appropriate to facilitating the lessons' activities.
3. Ensure that basic learning principles are well integrated into your plans.
4. Double-check your assessments of items one through three by asking a colleague or trusted friend to observe your instruction in terms of a formative evaluation model like the one described in Chapter 5.

3. *Q:* After reading this book, I'm amazed that a simple activity like teaching is so complex. I never thought there was so much to it. Does it have to be so sophisticated?

R: Teaching is an extremely sophisticated profession. It requires numerous cognitive and behavioral skills, many of which have been examined in this book. It is indeed a complex task to deal successfully day to day with the learning requirements of classes containing twenty-five to thirty-five pupils in light of the numerous educational demands of contemporary society. It requires a high level of professional maturity and skill. The successful teacher is probably one of society's most skilled professionals. It often seems strange to me that this truth is not recognized more widely. Most of us are fully prepared to acknowledge the complex skills of many professionals, but for some reason we are more reluctant to acknowledge the complex, sophisticated skills of those who provide the essential opportunities for the skill acquisition and training of others. Perhaps this unfortunate attitude is nowhere better exemplified than in the saying that graces almost every teacher training experience from time to time: "Those who can, do; those who can't, teach." Such uninformed biases give the erroneous impression that anyone can teach. However, although most people can have children, many fail in the complex task of being a parent; so, too, can many teachers enter a classroom and fail completely in the complex task of teaching.

This book has attempted to indicate specifically the cognitive and behavioral skills and strategies required for effective mastery of instruction. Complexity merely for the sake of complexity is, of course, to be abhorred. Complexity that results from specific analytic treatment of an extremely complex process, however, is necsssary in order not to mislead those who wish to acquire skills. Because something is complex does not mean that it cannot be mastered. However, it will not be mastered if its basic complexity is denied.

SUGGESTED ACTIVITIES

1. Outline a short curriculum unit (three to four lessons) for a specific subject and grade level of your choosing. After you have developed the unit outline, develop two of the lessons in detail using the total instructional planning format described in this chapter.

2. Reflect on the issue of teacher professionalism. Are teachers professionals? If so, what unique professional skills and abilities do teachers possess? What can individual teachers do to enhance their professional image?

REFERENCES

Bandura, A. 1977. *Social Learning Theory*. Englewood Cliffs, N.J.: Prentice-Hall.

Bandura, A. 1978. The Self System in Reciprocal Determinism. *American Psychologist* 33: 344–358.

Cohen, L., and Manion, L. 1977. *A Guide to Teaching Practice*. London: Methuen.

Native Indian Teacher Education Program. 1979. *NITEP Student Teaching Seminar Materials*. Faculty of Education, University of British Columbia, Vancouver, B.C.

Popham, W.J., and Baker, E.L. 1970. *Systematic Instruction*. Englewood Cliffs, N.J.: Prentice-Hall.

Index